P9-DNE-236

Praise for

Some Kind of Crazy

"Too often there's a giant chasm between what we believe about God and what we experience in life. That's true whether you're a Christian or you don't believe in God at all. Terry's utterly honest, surprising, and powerful personal story fuses those two disparate worlds together like no other book I've read. If you want to know where God is in the painful reality of your life, *Some Kind of Crazy* is a must-read."

—Carey Nieuwhof, author and founding pastor of Connexus Church

"Telling the entire truth of our lives is painfully difficult if we take the task seriously. To flourish, we must tell our stories truly—in all their longing, grief, pathos, and joy—for the entirety of our story to meet the one true Storyteller. He is the One who heals, convicts, and liberates us to live the lives he intended for us to live before the foundation of the world. With *Some Kind of Crazy,* Terry Wardle has given us the great gift of telling his story truly so that we might do the same. I cannot say it strongly enough: read this book, know the Truth, and discover your life of liberation and grace."

—Curt Thompson, MD, author of *The Soul of Shame* and *Anatomy of the Soul*

"*Some Kind of Crazy* is raw and funny, and it will capture your heart. I couldn't put the book down! Terry's real-life story is worth a thousand sermons because it demonstrates the possibility of God's amazing grace in your own life. This book is a powerful invitation to freedom from shame, performance, and failure."

—Dr. Juli Slattery, author of *Rethinking Sexuality*

"Many of us tend to compartmentalize—or worse yet, bury—the traumatic events of our past, failing to acknowledge the havoc they wreak on our present and future. In doing so, we bypass sacred opportunities for true freedom, lasting peace, and eternal significance. In Terry's honest, vulnerable recounting, we glimpse not only his rugged trek through early life brokenness and pain in pursuit of healing and wholeness but our own as well. Every soul cries out for the divine love that can mend its deepest wounds, and, as this book reveals with vivid clarity, none who seek are denied."

—Peter Burgo, editor, *Alliance Life* magazine

"It has been said that the life of faith is one of practicing, lapses, failures, and returning. And I've always thought that *returning* was the critical part. At its heart, Terry Wardle's astonishingly honest and inspiring book is about returning and returning and returning again to the Father, who waits with outstretched arms. So if you're starting to think your lapses and failures have left you too far from God, *this is the book for you*!"

—Sandra D. Wilson, PhD, spiritual director; retired family therapist and seminary professor; author of six books, including *Released from Shame* and *Into Abba's Arms*

"A rare book indeed! *Some Kind of Crazy* is simultaneously readable, scandalously authentic, and deeply emotional. About halfway through my journey with Terry in this book, I realized he isn't merely telling his story. He is helping me understand my wounds while positioning me for a healing experience with our Lord Jesus Christ! This memoir is like a light shining into the darkness for those who want to find a healing path."

—Rev. Canon Daniel W. Hardin, Anglican priest, military chaplain, and licensed marriage and family therapist

"Terry Wardle mines his own brokenness to show us how we, too, can be restored by God's redemptive grace and healing. You hold in your hand a valuable gift. I am grateful for his insights, wisdom, honesty, and sense of humor born out of his own life and faith. I am grateful."

—Ruth Graham, author of *Forgiving My Father, Forgiving Myself: An Invitation to the Miracle of Forgiveness*

"Terry Wardle tells an amazing story of his harrowing journey through abuse, paralyzing fear, and a desperate search for healing and grace. For the many thousands of people who have been deeply blessed by his writings and conferences on formational prayer, this moving book tells the backstory to his powerful ministry. For others, Terry's testimony can open a door to their own healing journey."

—Leonard Allen, dean, College of Bible & Ministry, Lipscomb University, Nashville, and author of *Poured Out: The Spirit of God Empowering the Mission of God*

SOME KIND OF CRAZY

An Unforgettable Story of Profound Brokenness and Breathtaking Grace

TERRY WARDLE

WATERBROOK

Some Kind of Crazy

Details in some anecdotes and stories have been changed to protect the identities of the persons involved.

This book is not intended to replace the medical advice of a trained medical professional. Readers are advised to consult a physician or other qualified health-care professional regarding treatment of their medical problems. The author and publisher specifically disclaim liability, loss, or risk, personal or otherwise, which is incurred as a consequence, directly or indirectly, of the use or application of any of the contents of this book.

Hardcover ISBN 978-0-525-65345-5
eBook ISBN 978-0-525-65346-2

Cover design by Mark D. Ford

Published in the United States by WaterBrook, an imprint of Random House, a division of Penguin Random House LLC.

Library of Congress Cataloging-in-Publication Data
Names: Wardle, Terry, author.
Title: Some kind of crazy : an unforgettable story of profound brokenness and breathtaking grace / by Terry Wardle.
Description: First Edition. | Colorado Springs : WaterBrook, 2019.
Identifiers: LCCN 2019000627| ISBN 9780525653455 (hardcover) | ISBN 9780525653462 (electronic)
Subjects: LCSH: Wardle, Terry. | Christian biography—United States.
Classification: LCC BR1725.W324 A3 2019 | DDC 277.3/082092 [B]—dc23
LC record available at https://lccn.loc.gov/2019000627

Printed in Canada
2019—First Edition

10 9 8 7 6 5 4 3 2 1

Contents

To Cheryl
and the day you said, "I do"

Prologue

I am a man who shouldn't be writing his story—the son of a coal miner whose hardscrabble family included a grandfather with a predilection for blowing up houses and sleeping with any woman who would half agree and a mother whose mission seemed focused on making her son into the most fearful man on the planet. Little wonder I ended up in a psychiatric hospital before the age of forty.

For my dad the family legacy was one of disdain, ridicule, abuse, and regret. For me it was a truckload of fear that followed me no matter where I went or what I accomplished.

There were amazing characters,* like Uncle Fred, known to the family as Uncle Fat due to the rolls of flesh that flowed over his belt and settled like a small mountain above his knees. Though Uncle Fat was the jolliest of men, in my last memory of him, he was in an alleyway sleeping off another hard-drinking night. The trouble was poor old Fat never woke up.

As a young boy growing up in the Appalachian coalfields of southwestern Pennsylvania, I had no idea that there could be better ways to live. Like other families in the area, mine was poor but not dirt poor, and there was no shame in it, at least not in the economic sense. Despite its craziness, I loved my family, regardless of the ways it wounded me.

---

* A few names have been changed to cloak the identities of those who appear in my story.

But what does a man whose life was shaped by an often affectionate, sometimes hilarious, and always dysfunctional family have to talk about? How is it possible that the life he has lived has any bearing on other lives, on your life, for instance?

By telling my story, I hope to explore what can happen not just in one life but in every life that is touched by the hand of God. Mine is a book that zeroes in on one life—on my life—in order to place the spotlight where it belongs—on the transformative journey from broken to beloved that begins whenever people put their hands into God's hand and allow him to take them wherever they need to go.

The story I tell begins with brokenness and pain. It's a journey of long duration. But its trajectory, its narrative arc, leans toward joy. By sharing my journey and the things God has taught me along the way, I hope to help you on your own transformative journey so that you can experience the richness of the life God has for you.

Because of my experience counseling, teaching, and praying with thousands of people over the course of many years, I have come to understand that it is only by looking back that we can begin to move forward on the healing path.

One

BROKEN

I once asked my dad if anyone had ever called us hillbillies. "If they ever dared to, I guarantee they'd never try it a second time," he said. "After a guy in a grocery store called your grandma white trash, Grandpap beat him out the door and down the steps in two seconds flat."

"'Course it wasn't like Grandpap was trying to stick up for her," he chuckled. "He'd probably been cheating on her the night before. He just didn't like some guy calling *his* woman white trash."

My grandfather was a rough and ruddy character, a short man whose face was littered with freckles that spilled down his neck and onto his muscular arms. With ice-blue eyes set close above a large nose red from years in the sun, he smelled of diesel fuel and dirt. Despite his rough edges, Grandpap could be pleasant, charming even, until somebody triggered him. When that happened, look out!

Life in Venetia, a hamlet in the southwestern corner of Pennsylvania, was never easy, especially for coal miners whose labor was both brutish and backbreaking. Every year the mine claimed its tithe of men. Those who survived formed a union and then walked off the job in protest, setting up picket lines that quickly turned into battle lines that soon became violent.

I'll never forget what happened to Ol' Man Barns, who lived in a three-room shack perched on the edge of a hill just above the railroad tracks. His worn-out patch of dirt couldn't produce enough food to feed his wife and kids, so when the owners of the Slopjar Mine dangled a small bonus in front of anyone who would cross the picket line, poor Ol' Barns took the bait.

Grandpap was furious when he heard the news. Like every other coal miner in our one-intersection town, he was 100 percent behind the strike. Barns was a *scab*, a *traitor*, and every infernal name Grandpap could think to call him. Clad in his favorite wifebeater T-shirt and a pair of grease-stained work pants, Grandpap paced the living room. Back and forth he stomped, running calloused hands through his reddish-brown hair, cussing a blue streak, and threatening that he was going to make Ol' Barns pay.

It must have been something to witness the white-hot curses that flew from his mouth like great bolts of lightning and the blue-tinged veins that bulged from his unwashed neck.

As Grandpap raged on about Barns's treachery, bitter winds blew through cracks in the rotted siding of my grandparents' not-so-snug home. Even the roaring fire couldn't fend off the chill that filled their shack that night.

But there was another fire burning—the one in Grandpap's gut. As his anger grew red hot, it forced him out of the house and into the darkness. His plan was simple enough. Head to the mine, break into the toolshed, and grab a stick of dynamite and a fuse. Thus armed, he would climb the wooded hill to Ol' Man Barns's house, where he would teach that scab a lesson he would never forget.

Confident no one could see him under the cover of night, Grandpap lit the fuse and then tossed the dynamite beneath the shabby porch that ran across the front of the old house.

Moments later, the porch disintegrated and a section of the house blew up. The blast was so powerful it propelled Mrs. Barns onto the top of the kitchen stove and laid her husband out cold on the living room floor.

Satisfied that it was a deed well done and in secret, Grandpap made his way back home through the night and settled beside Grandma on the couch, smugly confident that she was none the wiser about his nighttime errand.

But there were limits to Grandpap's brilliance. Like bread crumbs left by a child to mark his way home, his footprints in the snow led the police straight to his house. The cops followed his size nines right to the front door and arrested him on the spot, ignoring his vigorous protests of innocence. Couldn't they see he had been sitting with his wife on the couch the whole night?

Despite the evidence, Grandpap was acquitted on a technicality, which many surmise was the result of money changing hands. How Grandpap blew up Ol' Man Barns's house soon became part of the local lore, etching itself into our family history.

Grandpap and the Wardle Clan

People say that an apple always falls close to the tree. That was certainly the case when it came to Grandpap. His father, my great-grandfather, was an English outlaw by the name of Edwin Wardle, who, after serving time in prison, immigrated to America, leaving his wife and two children behind. Living with members of his mother's family, Edwin soon got his cousin Annie pregnant and then married her, despite the fact that he still had a family in England.

Together Annie and Edwin Wardle bought a farm in Venetia, in the middle of the Appalachian coalfields. Their marriage produced eight children, one of whom was Howard, or Howd, as Grandpap was called.

Howd and his brothers had two career choices—farming or coal mining. My grandpap chose the latter. All but one of his siblings stayed in Venetia, raising large families that were fiercely loyal to each other.

The Wardle clan was colorful and unpredictable with my grandpap being the most unpredictable of them all. By today's standards he would have been labeled a sex addict and a repeat offender. Back then people said he had a "way with the women" or that he was given to "sowing wild oats."

In 1925 when he was eighteen, Howd got a sixteen-year-old girl by the name of Bessie Murdy pregnant. She was later known to me as Grandma Mose. The two quickly married and then set up housekeeping in a neighborhood known as Bedbug Row. On the first day of June in 1926, my father was born. They named him, of course, Howard.

Both my grandparents were hot tempered and unyielding, which made for a fiery relationship. Disagreements would erupt into fights in which fists and frying pans would frequently fly. Inevitably, these arguments left soul-deep scars. After four chaotic years and one more child, they called it quits. Then my grandparents went their separate, irresponsible ways while their children were given to neighbors to raise.

Six years later Grandpap married an unsuspecting widow by the name of Matilda Yankeste Hardinger. We called her Grandma Til. But that was a loveless marriage too.

Like a child looking for someone to blame when things went wrong, Grandpap fingered my dad, saying he was the reason he had to marry two women he never loved. To young Puz, as my dad was called, the message was crystal clear—his daddy never wanted him.

Still, Howd found a use for his son. He started taking him out of school when he was only twelve years old, for two or three days a week, so he could help work Howd's wildcat coal mine. While other kids were getting an education, my father was breathing coal dust and loading a pit car by hand. Meanwhile, his father was off carousing with married women whose husbands had gone off to work.

An equal-opportunity offender, Grandpap cheated on both his wives. Grandma Til used to drive through town, going house to house trying to catch him out. To show his displeasure at her distrust, Grandpap simply muscled his motorcycle into the living room and then changed the oil on her new carpet.

One day while he was hammering to free a broken bolt on a bulldozer, the top of the punch mushroomed and a piece of metal flew off and lodged in his eye. The local doctor did his best to remove the splinter of metal but missed something. As the sliver moved deeper, the infection grew so severe that my grandfather had to have his left eye removed. Being fitted with a glass eye opened the door to the sick humor for which he was already famous.

Grandpap's favorite trick was to order a sandwich at a diner and then call out to the waitress, complaining that there was something wrong with his lunch. "This sandwich is looking at me," he would shout, every patron startled by his sudden outburst.

As the waitress hurried to the table, he would lift the top piece of bread and there it was—a big blue eyeball staring straight out of the ham and swiss! The waitress would shriek, and everyone at the table would laugh. Once again, my grandfather was the star of his very own three-ring circus.

Despite Grandpap's bad behavior, members of my family recall tales of Howd with genuine endearment. To relatives he was the Robin Hood of Venetia, though no one seemed to recall that he stole from both the rich and the poor, robbing his immediate family most of all.

A Darker Side

Though Grandpap had a talent for making people laugh and women swoon, he couldn't keep his dark side hidden for long. I encountered it for the first time when I was four years old.

One night as the summer sun was setting, I watched as eerie shadows danced across the living room floor of my grandparents' home. On hands and knees near Grandma Til's feet, I was busy galloping plastic horses across the floorboards. Roy Rogers and the

Lone Ranger had already convinced me there was but one true path for a man, and that was to be a cowboy.

Though I loved my grandparents, I felt unsettled in their house, with its musty furniture, dimly lit rooms, and the old coal furnace that belched black soot and made anyone who opened the boiler door look like the devil himself. Neither did I manage to get used to the freight train that shook the house twice daily, rumbling past less than fifty feet from the back door.

That evening, the screen door screeched open, then slapped shut with a familiar finality. I hurried to the dining room to see if Mom or Dad had come to pick me up. But it was only Grandpap. My heart sank a little as I went back to Grandma Til's feet to help my horses gallop across the hardwood prairie.

"Are you hungry, Howd?" asked Grandma. "I can warm dinner for you."

After a long silence, Grandpap said, "Terry, let's you and me go for a ride in the country."

I turned and looked at Grandma Til. Though her face registered surprise, with a gentle smile she nodded her approval.

Grandpap lifted me to my feet and led me through the front door, off the tall porch, and around to the back of the house where his 1952 Chrysler Imperial was parked. He opened the door, hiked me up on the passenger seat, and then went around to the driver's side. Nothing was said as he started the engine and backed onto the grass in the side yard.

Slowly, he drove up the long gravel driveway that ran between the house and McConnahay's Country Store. Then he made a quick right turn onto Mingo Creek Road. Still not a word was spoken. As we traveled in silence through the countryside and then turned onto a wagon path that led into the woods, an ugly feeling swept over me.

The car crept into the forest, branches scratching against the side panels as though the trees that pressed so close were trying to catch and hold us. Witches screaming threats could not have frightened me more than those sounds as we kept driving forward on that path. What happened next haunted me for decades.

Grandpap stopped the car in a small hollow far from the road so that we were invisible to cars or people walking by. By now the sun had set and the trees were casting shifting shadows, their limbs moving back and forth in the wind. My four-year-old brain went into overdrive as I imagined strangers emerging from the trees or wild animals that would eat me alive. I wanted to scream for my mother. But I couldn't. I was frozen.

"Terry, get in the back and hide on the floor." Grandpap ordered.

I turned cold as ice and began to shake. I couldn't move.

"Terry, I told you to get in the back seat and hide." Grandpap grabbed me by the arm and pushed me over the seat and into the back.

Why do I need to hide? Are people going to hurt me? What's wrong? These were the questions I wanted to scream at him, but I couldn't get the words out. Instead I stood on the floor in the back, transfixed as Grandpap reached for the glove box.

That's when I saw him pull out a worn leather holster cradling a revolver with a barrel the size of a cannon. I could see the anger on his face as he turned to me again and said, "I told you to get down on the floor. Do you hear me? Don't make a sound."

As I cowered on the floor, he repeated, "Just be quiet!"

Then he got out of the car and slammed the door. The sound of the door closing behind him and my grandfather's fading footsteps turned that four-door sedan into a jail cell. In the blackness I lay trembling, inhaling dust from the floor mats beneath me. As my mind raced uncontrollably, my throat began to constrict and I could hardly breathe. Chills swept over me that even a hot summer night could not dispel.

A small boy caught in a nightmare, I got on my knees, placing my face on the back seat. To soothe myself, I began rubbing my hands back and forth across the soft velour seat covers, tears streaming down my cheeks. "Please help me, please help me, please help me," I whispered. But there was nobody there to hear my pleas.

The panic I felt in the car that night was sustained by the sound of trees moaning in the wind and the sensation of the car rocking ever so slightly. I had no idea whether my grandfather would ever return or whether I would even survive the night. The terror I felt in that single hour would mar my life for years to come.

Finally I heard footsteps approaching through the dark. Closing my eyes against the moment when a stranger would break into the car and grab me, I was surprised when the door jerked open and there stood Grandpap, winded and covered in sweat. Jumping into the driver's seat, he stuffed the revolver back into the glove box and started the engine.

I felt relieved and angry at the same time. Young as I was, I knew he had wronged me. The very person who should have protected me had terrorized me instead.

As Grandpap leaned back over the seat, backing through the woods and onto Mingo Creek Road, he said nothing. Still shaking, I climbed off the floor and onto the back seat. When we reached his house, I was relieved to see my parents' tan-and-white Mercury parked out front. Still sweating, Grandpap stopped the car and turned to me. "This will be our little secret," he said.

Unable to sleep that night, I told my parents everything that had happened. But they brushed it off, as though I had made up the whole thing. Because neither of them promised to keep me safe or helped me process the experience, which might have enabled me to understand what had happened, I relived the nightmare over and over throughout my childhood. It was years before my father finally admitted he had believed every word I'd said. He knew exactly what Grandpap had been up to that night, though he never bothered to confront him about it.

The wagon path Grandpap had turned onto that summer evening ran through the woods above Blanche and Harold Collins's house. Harold worked second shift at the strip mine and always left the house around two in the afternoon, leaving his wife alone. Whenever he was away, Blanche was only too happy to welcome Grandpap into her loving arms. Of course, the gun he had taken with him was insurance, just in case Harold came home at an inconvenient time.

No wonder Grandpap had invited me to come along. My role was to be a ruse, throwing my grandmother off track so that he could satisfy his insatiable appetite for immorality.

Because our family lived by the "no talk" rule, everybody looked the other way when I told them what had happened. As a result, the emotional wounding I experienced that night festered deep inside, contributing to the chronic anxiety and fear that would come to characterize my life.

Being a Wardle meant so many things. Most importantly, it meant you were supposed to suck things up and move on down the road. I learned that lesson well, eventually pushing the event as far out of my mind as possible. I didn't know that minimizing what had happened to me that night was a way of cooperating with the emotional downfall that would surely come.

More Gunplay

After Grandpap's little escapade, I had a hard time sleeping. As long as I could hear Mom and Dad awake in the living room, I was fine. But once they turned off the lights and the house fell silent, fear would grab me by the throat and make it hard to breathe. Alone in the dark, I would turn on the lights to see if anyone had sneaked into my room, at which point Mom would yell at me to turn them off.

Once, in the early hours of the morning, I couldn't stop fretting. Without turning on the lights, I began creeping down the long, dark hallway to my parents' bedroom. If I could make it to the safety of their bed, I knew that no monsters could ever find me.

Sliding both hands across the plaster wall to guide me, I inched my way across the hardwood floor, moving as silently as possible. I didn't want my parents to wake up and order me back to my room.

Suddenly the hall light switched on. A pistol was pointed at me, just inches from my face!

Though he was upset to find he'd pulled a gun on his own son after mistaking me for a robber, my dad had no idea how traumatized I was. The scene would have been laughable, at least to some, had it not happened to a young boy who had already suffered his share of trauma. I was only five years old when that second terrifying encounter with a gun happened.

Later, I wondered why the Wardle clan was always so worried about robbers. Not one thing was ever stolen from our home, nor did a single person ever break in to harm anyone. But Dad kept a loaded gun with him in the house. Like most of our relatives, he had a gun case full of ammunition and shotguns. There was an irony in all of this because the Wardles were the ones with all the guns. If anyone was going to break the law, it would probably be one of us.

Grandpap's Last Gift

Though Grandpap had lost his eye, the surgeon had missed at least one sliver of metal. All the while my grandfather had been busy carousing and playing jokes on waitresses, that little bit of metal had been traveling deeper into his head until it finally formed an abscess in his brain. On a wintery day in December, we all discovered the problem at the same time.

I was in the kitchen with Grandma Til when I heard the first bloodcurdling scream. Trembling as I backed against the box freezer, I stared as Grandma ran out of the kitchen and into the dining room.

Soon Grandpap came stumbling in with Grandma propping him up on one side and Aunt Peg on the other. They were headed to the bathroom. But they never got there. Moaning loudly, he fell on the linoleum floor just feet from where I was standing.

"Howd, what's wrong?" Grandma screamed. "Get up, Howd, get up!" Fighting furiously to get him to the bathroom, she cried out his name over and over. But Grandpap just lay there.

I had no idea that my fifty-year-old grandfather had just suffered a cerebral hemorrhage and that he had gone into a coma from which he would not emerge.

Since my parents didn't take me to his funeral, it seemed as though Grandpap had simply disappeared. But not all of him. Something still lingered. After I watched him collapse in agony, the night terrors I had been battling got worse. Whenever darkness fell and I lay alone in my bedroom, I worried that I would die in agony just like Grandpap. Night after night I would lie awake begging for dawn to come.

Surprisingly, my parents never made the connection between the traumas I had suffered in quick succession and the fear I constantly battled. Over time, Mom simply labeled me a "nervous child," while Dad thought of me as a "sissy."

Those childhood woundings, the first of many, fractured my heart in a way that made me afraid of my own shadow. I was ready to flee or to fight no matter how slight the threat.

My dad always said Grandpap could have been a millionaire if he had been able to keep his pants up. Well, he couldn't, so poverty was what remained for Grandma Til. Of course, Grandpap did leave behind an inheritance of sorts, especially for my father. He left Dad a coal-truck load of insignificance bulldozed into his life for thirty years. He did that by communicating a steady stream of ridicule and abuse and by blaming him for the results of his own bad behavior.

Someone once asked if I felt relieved when Grandpap died. Not at all. He was my grandfather. Despite the fact that he had wounded me, like all the characters in the story of my life, I loved him. He was an impulsive, immoral man who was larger than life and notoriously charming. The truth is I miss him. I wish he had lived a long life, had taken me on great adventures, and had bought me the horse he promised and my first deer rifle. If he had lived, I might have had my own car when I turned sixteen, learned how to drive a steam shovel, and seen him waving at me in the crowd at my ball games. Had he lived, I might also have ended up more like him than I care to admit.

Only by reflecting from the distance of time have I been able to see that there was something crazy important about his story for me.

Two

AT THE RIVER

The Wardle clan ran on a set of tracks that headed into territory few other families dared or desired to go. We had our own set of unspoken rules that guided our journey through life. Rule number one was to disdain education because too much schooling could ruin a man. Rule number two was to stay away from church because religion would turn us into weaklings. Rule number three was to obey the law but only when it was convenient to do so. Fun-loving, gun-toting, bed-hopping, larger-than-life, law-breaking rascals—that was how many people saw us.

As crazy as the Wardle values were, I loved my family and the place where I was raised. That tiny corner of a less sophisticated world still has its hooks in me.

I find contentment remembering the people who lived there, families with last names like Devore, Durham, Campbell, Lash, McChesney, Higbee, and even Hatfield, a distant branch of that infamous feuding family. I am proud that my roots are connected to hard-living people who built simple homes in wooded hollows along polluted streams flowing through hillsides that still bore the scars of strip mining.

But memories can be like steep slopes of the same hill. Many of the things I remember about my life generate shame as well as affection, not only from what I did and saw but especially from what was done to me.

Because of that, home is the place that calls me back and the place I fight so frantically to leave behind.

My children can hardly believe the stories I tell. My son once said that folks on the Wardle side of the family with names like Carrot, Coon Dog, Puz, Uncle Hooks, Aunt Chubb, Mose, Uncle Fat, and Bull Chicken sound more like cartoon characters than real people. But these were the flesh-and-blood family members who populated every day of my early life.

No one was closer than Grandma Mose, Grandpap's first wife and my dad's mom. After divorcing Grandpap, she married a man whose nickname was Mose. Every day, multiple times a day, I walked next door to the love and madness dwelling within the four walls of their home. A big woman with a big heart, Grandma Mose always opened her door to displaced relatives with lifestyles that made the neighbors blush. None more so than her brother, my Uncle Fat.

Fat's mouth was often stained with residue from a baseball-sized chaw of Mail Pouch tobacco bulging in his right cheek. He wore pants that looked like they were fighting his belly, which busted through his flannel shirt like a pig poking through an old wood fence. His head was bald, and his face was red from years dedicated to the bottle.

Though Uncle Fat lived with Grandma Mose, he would disappear for days on end. Sooner or later the police would show up with the news that Fat was drying out down at the station. Sometimes Grandma Mose would send Dad out looking for him before the cops picked him up. On one expedition we discovered him in a shack in the woods, sleeping on the floor with a bunch of other bad-smelling men.

Though Fat was notorious for his benders, I loved being with him. What boy wouldn't like spending time with a jolly, fun-loving uncle who taught him to cuss by the time he was three? He got me to memorize little poems filled with bad words. Whenever folks stopped by, he would have me recite those verses and then throw back his head in toothless hilarity. I loved watching his belly shake and the way his face turned blue as he laughed. And I enjoyed the soft wheezy sounds he made, reminding me of the noises one of my cousins made during an asthma attack.

Even as a kid I knew my family was different. I understood they did things that could get them into trouble with the police. Grandpap had been arrested a few times and chased through town more than once when trying to make a trade with some housewife—a load of coal for a romp in the hay. More often than not he made the sale. I knew the men in my family drank and had tried their hand at distilling whiskey during the Depression. I also knew they ignored every hunting regulation ever written and that they were known more for fighting than being faithful.

At least we were not racists. That was a point of pride for me. Because we were from the wrong side of the tracks, we interacted with people of color every day and, as far as I could remember, treated them with respect. I had best friends who were black, I went to integrated schools, and I had black roommates in college. My relatives may have bent the law and lived rowdy lives but at least they weren't prejudiced, or so I thought. But that particular balloon popped the day my dad dropped the news that my favorite uncle—Uncle Fat—was a "card-carrying" member of the KKK.

As a young woman, Grandma Mose had been wild, unrestrained, and undisciplined, a force of nature that backed down from no one. She was kicked out of school for beating up her teacher. Later she beat up her boss and lost her job. Once she even jumped a four-foot fence to rip into a neighbor who had said something disparaging about my dad.

After her brief marriage to Grandpap, which included unfaithfulness all around, she solidified her reputation for hard living by running around with various men. When I asked my father if his mother had been a prostitute, he hesitated and then said, "I can't say, but I know she sure gave a lot of it away."

My grandmother's second husband was a much younger man by the name of Adam Lilly, whom everyone called Mose. He never had much to do with me, leaving the house every evening at six o'clock to chase away his blues with bottles of Iron City Beer.

Despite her colorful reputation, I have nothing but the best memories of Grandma Mose. Every day, until the day I went away to college, she greeted me warmly in a worn-out cotton dress that barely concealed her ample flesh. Though she had false teeth up and down, she wore them only on Fridays because that was her day for playing bingo at the Moose Lodge, which she did with the faithfulness of a nun attending mass. Often there was a rub of snuff tucked behind her bottom lip. She also took a nip of whiskey here and there. Though she wasn't much of a smoker, I remember watching her roll a cigarette with one hand. Even into her nineties Grandma Mose ate more chips and chocolate than she ever did vegetables.

The first scent to greet me as I stepped through her door was vanilla. I would walk into the kitchen and see her with an apron wrapped around her large waist. Dough an inch thick would be spread out across the counter, and Grandma Mose would be cutting it to size with a Mason jar turned upside down. Next to the oven would be cooling racks filled with soft, fat sugar cookies.

"You want one, Bud?" she would always ask. As I brought a large warm cookie to my mouth, I breathed an aroma I have always associated with love. Her sugar cookies melted my anxieties away.

Grandma Mose's house was always jammed with family members. Whenever he wasn't lost in an alcoholic fog, Uncle Fat was there, sharing a room with his mother, my Great-Grandma Murdy, who had moved in after her husband's death. Then, when Uncle Will passed, Grandma Mose's sister Verda moved in. My Aunt Peg and my cousin Sandy shared the small back bedroom. I have no idea how they made ends meet on the meager wages Mose made working on the county road crew, but somehow Grandma Mose made it work.

There are other players who provided color to the landscape of my life. In some people's stories they would be seen as mere extras and bit actors who served as unnoticed scenery behind a greater personal narrative. In my case, these men and women contributed to what is the best and worst about me. Their presence shaped a great deal of what I grew to believe about myself, about other people, and about God.

Though Grandma's brother, my Uncle Bill, didn't live with her, he stopped by every day, often at mealtime. A notorious womanizer, Bill drove a beat-up black Cadillac purchased from the local undertaker. A tall, big-boned man, he was louder than usual whenever he had a drunk on, which was often.

Bill's favorite story was about how he gave the army the slip by intentionally wetting his cot. Night after night he just let the river run. According to the way he told the story, it seemed like the military gave out medals for such behavior. But instead of a medal, he got booted out with a dishonorable discharge. It was Bill who gave me my first handgun when I was only ten years old. I still have it.

One of Dad's cousins, a guy whose wife called him the Old Man, was married to a woman he called Chubb. Even as a young boy, I could see that Chubb and the Old Man didn't get along. One day, while the Old Man was asleep in his chair, Chubb poured alcohol over his bare feet. Did I mention he had athlete's foot? While Chubb looked on, the Old Man shot up out of his chair and began dancing across the living room floor, jumping up and down as though he had just set foot on the sun.

On another occasion Chubb was using hair spray when the end broke off and it started shooting out like a fire extinguisher. Holding the can over the toilet, she let the spray empty into the bowl. Later that day, the Old Man came in and sat down on the toilet while smoking a cigarette. He took one long drag, spread his legs, and then threw the cigarette into the toilet. The next thing Chubb heard was the Old Man peeling himself off the bathroom ceiling and calling for ice to soothe his backside.

One of my favorite relatives was Uncle Charlie. A tall, sinewy man with a bald head and large ears, he had hands the size of moonshine jugs, one of which was missing an index finger from a farm accident.

One day Charlie received a notice from the county that it was taking his land through the process of eminent domain to make room for a park that would be built there. When deputies arrived to evict him, he met them at the door with a shotgun. Refusing to leave his home, he informed them that he had planted nitro all across the farm. If they tried to take the land, he assured them, they would soon come face-to-face with their maker. It took two years and federal agents to evict Uncle Charlie and Aunt Alice. The Wardles never forgave the government for that.

We were nothing if not resilient. My dad's sister Peg had married a man named Frank. The two fought frequently. They would split up and get back together, split up and get back together. During one of their split-up times, Frank begged my Aunt Peg to take him back. To discuss the matter, she agreed to go for a ride with him in his car. But when she refused to let him back into her life, Uncle Frank became incensed, accusing her of seeing another man. Pulling out his handgun, he threatened to kill her if she didn't tell him who the scoundrel was. Then he shot her in the chest.

Though bleeding, Aunt Peg managed to open the car door and run for her life. Empty shell casings went flying through the air like hot metal confetti from his semiautomatic Colt as Uncle Frank chased after her, determined to finish her off.

Banging on a neighbor's door, Aunt Peg finally made it to safety. But by the time the police and the doctor arrived, she was bleeding out on their couch.

When my dad caught wind of what had happened, he and Uncle Fat grabbed for their guns and rushed to the scene. They were going to take Frank out. But by then my uncle was already sitting in the back of a police car. Enraged, Dad fought to get inside so he could kill Frank for what he had done to his sister.

Finally, the doctor called Dad and Uncle Fat into the house to deliver the sad news. There was no way my Aunt Peg would live through the night. He was sure she had been shot in the heart.

In the midst of this dark family episode, two surprising things happened. First, though her left breast had been shot off, Aunt Peg lived. In fact, she lived a long life and there was some happiness in it, especially when she came to faith.

Second, Uncle Frank was convicted of attempted murder and imprisoned for seven years. Though that wasn't surprising, I was shocked when he showed up at Grandma Mose's house after his release and took Aunt Peg and my cousin Sandy to live with him. Peg and Frank never lived apart again.

What surprised me even more was my father's attitude toward Uncle Frank. He acted as though nothing much had happened. My parents even vacationed with Frank and Peg at times. I couldn't understand how my dad, who had once tried to kill Frank for shooting his sister, had managed to make peace with him. I wanted to think there had been long talks, admissions of guilt, and forgiveness extended. But that was not the Wardle way.

My family never talked about it again and simply moved on as though nothing had ever happened. I saw the same kind of bizarre behavior when family members cheated on each other . . . with each other . . . and then went on as if nothing had happened. The only way I know to describe the whole thing is "crazy making."

The River

It was cold, the sky overcast and gray. The Ohio River flowed with frightening force, violently churning debris and mud from winter's thaw and spring rain. I stood mesmerized by the swift current, careful to keep my footing on the steep, rocky shore.

I was in Newburgh, Indiana, for my youngest daughter's wedding. In the early afternoon, I slipped away for a walk to the water's edge. Gazing at the rapidly moving river, I noticed a line of empty barges moving downstream, pushed by a paint-starved tugboat belching smoke.

The sight evoked memories from when I would lie in bed on hot summer nights, listening to the long, mournful sounds of the foghorns bellowing on the Monongahela River near my childhood home. Those warnings had always felt strangely comforting to a small boy lying wide awake in a dark and lonely room.

Coal was our family business, dug out in pitch darkness hundreds of feet below the Appalachian earth by my great-grandfather, grandfather, and father. I remember sitting on the riverbank watching long lines of rusty steel barges snaking their way down the river, filled with coal that had been plucked from the ground by people I knew.

Now I was standing at the Ohio River, entertaining memories that drew me back to the place where I grew up and the people who shaped much of the story that is my life. The narrative came alive as I stared at the teeming waters at my feet and thought about the past.

A gentle rain began to fall, and I felt a chill come over me. A cold breeze drafting across the river grew stronger, and the rocky bank became slick. The sun was softly setting behind the town, a reminder that I had stayed too long. I needed to go back and rejoin my family, but I was lost in another time and place.

I was quite undone on the banks of the Ohio River. Like the swiftly moving current churning up mud from the bottom, my mind had dredged up memories from the long-ago past, and with those memories had come pain from wounds that had not yet healed.

As I stared across the water to the south side of the river, I noticed a muddy bank that led to a wooded, tangled, unpopulated land. I began thinking of it as it must have been before the Civil War when African Americans had two totally different experiences of life depending on which side of the Ohio River they stood.

Across the river in Kentucky, less than a quarter mile away, men, women, and children were held as property, with no rights or privileges protected by law. They were mistreated at will, considered three-fifths human, and seen as chattel. Families were routinely torn apart by owners who often used Bible passages as justification for their vile and violent treatment.

As I was imagining the suffering these people had faced, an unexpected thought forced its way into my mind. What if some of the slaves had made the life-threatening journey across the Ohio, yet had spent their lives on freedom's side living by the same oppressive rules and bondage of slavery? What if they had lived without the joy of freedom? What if they had failed to understand that they were valued human beings who deserved to be protected and respected? Given what freedom cost, that would have been tragic.

"Living in bondage on freedom's side." Suddenly the phrase that popped into my head hit home. It seemed to perfectly describe my own journey. My early life had broken something inside me. First it was Grandpap and the fear he brought. Then it was living with a dad who was fighting to prove his manhood and a mom who couldn't attach to me. Then came all the years of growing up in a clan filled with addiction and violence.

Even though God reached out and took me by the hand when I was a teenager, I spent many years on freedom's side living in bondage. I was saved but not free. While I had the assurance of heaven, I often felt I was living in hell. No amount of performing for God touched the pain that gripped me.

Rather than fighting to distance myself from my home and the people who shaped me, I revisited them and the worst parts of my past.

Uncle Fat, Grandma Mose, Aunt Peg, Uncle Frank, Carrot, Coon Dog, Puz, Uncle Hooks, Chubb, and Bull Chicken. The alcoholism, the prejudice, the meanness, the lack of care, the craziness. Strange love wrapped in a ribbon of hate.

Friends urged me to run. For a while I tried to. But that never works. I have to tell the story. I have to follow the crooked path that led me straight to where I needed to go.

Three

MOTHER WOUNDS

I busted into the house clad only in gym shorts, a sweaty practice jersey, and the lingering scent of a boys' locker room. Exhausted from practicing basketball, I had only one thing on my mind. Food, glorious food! Bounding up the basement steps, I heard voices in the living room. I recognized one belonging to a favorite cousin whose nickname was Carrot and another belonging to his wife, Evelyn.

Though my dad said Carrot's nose grew longer with every story he told, I enjoyed the embellishments, which were as colorful as the thatch of orange hair sprouting from his scalp. If he wasn't breathlessly relating the story of an incredible deal he had just made or the prize-winning buck he had just bagged, Carrot was telling us what it felt like to drive the fastest car in town. A blue-collar Walter Mitty, he was an underachiever assigning himself an oversized role in the world. As an uneducated man who could neither read nor write, he must have yearned for the respect he never received.

Today Carrot was bragging about how he had connected with a "Chinaman" the night before on his radio set. Never mind that he couldn't speak a word of Chinese or that, like the rest of our family, he possessed not an ounce of racial sensitivity. He just kept spinning a yarn about the fascinating "Chinaman" he'd just befriended.

As I walked into the living room, I pulled out my report card, placed it on the mantel, and grabbed some snacks from the TV tray. Settling in to enjoy the rest of Carrot's improbable story, I failed to notice as my mother rose from her chair and walked toward the mantel where she picked up and opened my card.

While Carrot was still speaking, she began to chuckle. As her laughter continued, Carrot stopped talking and she started reading with dramatic effect:

"English, D.

"Arithmetic, D.

"Geography, C-.

"Listens Well, Unsatisfactory.

"Fulfills Assignments, Unsatisfactory.

"Punctuality, Satisfactory. I guess he got that one right."

Ending her responsive reading, she smiled at my dad, then at Carrot and Evelyn, and then at me. Closing the report card, she slid it back into the folder with the precision of a blaster inserting a fuse into a stick of dynamite. Placing it on the mantel, she patted it for effect. Then she walked back toward her seat and without glancing my way said, "It's all right, Terry; everyone knows you have horse---t for brains."

Carrot slapped his knee and nearly spit out his false teeth while Dad and Evelyn shook with laughter. Meanwhile, Mom stared at me with a satisfied grin on her face, as though to say she knew her words had found their target. This was more than an evaluation of my academic performance. It was a statement about my worth as a human being.

The more everyone laughed, the angrier I became. *Why now? Why did she have to do it in front of my cousins? Why spoil everything just when I was enjoying a rare happy moment in this house of horrors?*

I wanted to burn the house down. I wanted to scream at everyone to shut up! Instead I hung my head in shame. I was annihilated.

From then on, my mother's words hung like a toxic fog over everything I accomplished. Long after I had finished college and completed graduate school, I could still hear the laughter and see the look of disdain on her face. No matter what I achieved, it was never enough. I was a poser. Someday people would discover the truth—I had horse---t for brains.

Years passed before I brought the moment up to Mom, hoping she would understand how deeply she had hurt me. Instead of an apology there was only a quick retort. "I guess what I said helped," she said. "Look, you straightened up enough to finally be somebody." That was the end of the conversation.

"Don't Make a Mess!"

I learned early to fear my mother. That's the way Mom wanted it. Fear was her favorite behavioral tool, a way to control me. The mean look, the harsh remark, the quick movement from her chair toward the wooden spoon in the kitchen—these were all carefully staged. She was so good at it that she could invoke fear merely by clearing her throat.

With Mom there was never the sense that the punishment should fit the crime. Discipline was meted out not according to the scale of the offense but according to whether she and Dad had been arguing or whether she was in a good mood or a bad one. Her forceful brand of discipline left lasting impressions on both skin and soul.

Still, there were times when Mom could be gentle, affectionate, and affirming. But even when she was, I felt uneasy because I knew her love depended on variables I couldn't control. I also knew how quickly the wind could shift, how rapidly strings could be pulled. Like a cat that purrs at you one moment and then sinks a claw into you the next, Mom was unpredictable. Her volatility triggered my anxiety.

Of all the fear-inducing interactions I had with her, few were as complex as what took place whenever I became ill. I hated being sick because illness always meant enemas, and enemas meant pain and humiliation. Trouble followed if everything didn't go just right when the solution was being administered.

The routine was always the same. It didn't matter what ailed me. Sore stomach, sore throat, or a case of the sniffles, I had to strip off my clothes and lie down in a fetal position on the floor of our small bathroom.

Though the tile felt cold and damp against my skin, it was nothing compared to the humiliation that followed. Mom would begin by digging around in her enema kit for just the right size nozzle. It was useless to ask for one of the smaller ones. Then she would fill a hot water bottle with soapy water and hang it on the North Star. At least that's what it felt like when the water came rushing out of the hose and forcing its way into me.

"Don't you dare make a mess for me!" she would yell, all the while keeping the water flowing. If there was a mess, I had to join in on the cleanup, which only added to the nightmare.

The bathroom that served as the pump station was so tiny that the door had to stay open in order to fit my mother and me and the contraptions necessary to perform the procedure. Though my sister kept a safe distance lest she become the next victim, the open-door policy meant that Dad could wander by at any moment. His indifference to what my mother was doing both shamed and infuriated me.

As I grew older I realized that he was afraid of my mother. Perhaps he thought that if he protested, he would be next. I wondered what nozzle she would have used on him.

Years later, I ask myself what had driven my mother to insist on such an invasive procedure. Where did she get the idea this would help? How could she do such things to her children without a shred of compassion or empathy? Though there were situations in which Mom could be loving, she could also induce pain and remain unmoved and undeterred.

It took years for me to understand the relationship between the brutality she endured as a child and her own emotional disconnection. Something deep inside was so wounded that feelings of empathy were no longer accessible to her. Mom couldn't attune to what others were feeling and modulate her response accordingly. Anger could flow in her with a force that would both frighten and undo me.

As time went on, I fought hard to deny feeling ill. I also began to wonder why I got enemas instead of the ginger ale, Jell-O, or ice cream my friends enjoyed when they were sick. Instead of treating me with sympathy and kindness, assuring me I would feel better soon, my mother had devised a harsh bathroom ritual that made me associate illness with guilt and sickness with punishment. Little wonder that my wife once asked why I apologized whenever I felt ill.

I had simply assumed that frequent enemas were a part of everyone's life. As an adult, I was surprised to learn (and believe me, I have asked) that many people have no memory of their mother possessing a dark green box stuffed with a rubber water bottle, a hose, an array of nozzles, and a clip to hang the bottle from the bathroom shower rod. I guess they missed out.

Best Day, Worst Day

Some days are turning points. Mine came after six straight days of rain that gradually gave way to sunshine.

Cooped up in our tiny house made me feel as stir-crazy as a caged animal on display at the county fair. As I paced restlessly across the living room floor, my mother snapped at me. "Go to your room and play!" It didn't matter that my bedroom was the size of a walk-in closet. Step through the doorway, and it was either fall into bed or turn left and bang your knees into a chest of drawers. The storm of restlessness raging inside my ten-year-old brain threatened to blow me into a thousand pieces. It was either break out or break down, but something had to give.

Like the deluge story of Genesis, the rain finally stopped and the dove returned. The moment my mother said I could go outside, I bounded down the basement steps, grabbed my bike, and burst through the door to freedom.

My bike was a big blue Schwinn affair with fat whitewall tires and an old set of saddlebags attached to the rear fender by my alcoholic step-grandfather. It was his attempt to preserve my masculinity as I rode a girl's bike through the neighborhood.

Peddling frantically across our flat driveway, I picked up speed to scale the hill to my friend's house. Climbing the steep gravel road that was Norman Avenue, I stood on the peddles, pushing with all my strength to gain momentum. At the crest of the hill, I turned left and glided into Kenny Bruznak's driveway. He was on his knees staring at a toad trapped in a window well.

Kenny and I walked to Gastonville Elementary, a mile down the hill from my house. During the summer, we teamed up for adventures in the woods behind the grade school. I was tall for my age, skinny, with jet-black hair mowed short as fuzz. Kenny was shorter, carried a bit of weight, and had yellow wisps of hair that he was forever brushing from his eyes.

In the blink of an eye, we were racing down Don Street, headed for the section of our neighborhood the kids called Snake Hill. New houses were being built, which meant heavy equipment and an inexhaustible supply of scrap wood thrown aside by carpenters. It was a boy's paradise.

Six days of rain had chased the construction workers home so the place was ours. The downpour had turned the newly bulldozed hillside into a mudslide running with water. It flowed down the steep bank and emptied into a pit knee deep in muck. Some things in life do not demand thoughtful consideration. This was one.

Kenny and I spent the best morning of my boyhood laughing and sliding all over that hillside. Not a single grown-up ever broke into view, leaving us as free as Huck Finn and Tom Sawyer. We slid down forward, backward, upside down, and flat on our bellies. We were caked in mud from head to toe. All my anxious cares were cleansed in a baptism of rain-soaked Snake Hill earth. I had arrived a boy, but was leaving an unrecognizable earth creature, returned to primal good, clean dirt! I never felt more like me.

When Kenny's mom saw us turn into the driveway, she laughed until she cried. There was comfort in her smile, awakening something I had experienced few times before. Feeling safe even in the midst of mischief and mud, I could have stayed in that sublime moment forever.

While Mrs. Bruznak ran warm baths for both of us, we headed to the basement to peel off our clothes. I can still hear the sound of my shirt slapping the floor under the weight of all that mud, Kenny and I reliving every filthy moment we spent together.

I had soaked in a tub before, but this was different. The water was deep, not just a skim over the bottom of the porcelain. It felt warm and soft against my naked skin. Kenny's mom discretely handed towels, underwear, pants, and a shirt into the bathroom. Not one cross word, no rebuke for the mess, only gentle-humored understanding. She was the prettiest mother I had ever seen.

Holding tightly to every moment as if each second were a step toward heaven itself, I didn't want to leave. Dressed in Kenny's clothes, I watched as his mom stuffed all my muddy belongings into a large paper bag and then sent me on my way with a peck on the cheek. Cruising down the hill to our driveway, I was as content as I had ever been. Surely this was the best day of my life.

Entering through the side door, bag in hand, I found my mother and my sister together in the kitchen. Noticing I was dressed in someone else's clothes, Mom demanded an explanation. I smiled, eager to tell her about my day. Instead of returning my smile, she lunged at me, ripping the bag of dirty clothes from my hands. As she looked inside and then up at me, the glare in her eyes sent chills across my body.

"You did what?" she screamed. "You got your clothes caked in mud? You went to the neighbor's house and took a bath? Are you that stupid? Now I have to wash *your* clothes and the Bruznak kid's as well? Get to the basement."

As I started down the stairs, she exploded with uncontrollable rage, beating me down the steps and screaming in my face, "All you ever do is make work for me!" She swung the heavy bag of wet clothes like someone swatting bees, slapping it against my head and back. When the bag broke, sending wet clothes flying down the steps, she grabbed a broom.

I blocked the blows as best I could, but a broom is hard to resist. Stinging welts formed on my arms and hands as I fought to get away. No matter where I ran or how fast I went, she locked on with laser precision. With every blow she kept yelling, "Maybe that will teach you!"

I didn't cry. I didn't dare fight back. I was just struggling to survive. But in the midst of flailing arms and brutal words, I felt the power of hate.

Late that night, pulling the covers over my head, I began to sob. How was it that my perfect day had turned into the worst day of all? I felt a jumble of grief and hurt, scared, confused, and angry. Though the bruises stung, the pain was nothing compared to the wound laid open in my heart.

Night terrors soon leaked into my daytime hours, and I began to feel as unsafe on the inside as I did on the outside. It wasn't long until my body gave voice to what I was too frightened to say. Battles with chronic eczema and bouts of shingles were met with remedies that were only skin deep. The adults in my world failed to notice that I was a child dancing on the edge of darkness.

Four

CRAZY FAITH

Like vinegar and oil, the Wardles and church didn't mix, at least not for long. As far as I know, none of my grandparents or great-grandparents ever belonged to a church. Though Dad had allowed his children to be baptized in the privacy of the local pastor's living room, he was certain the roof would collapse if he so much as set a toe into a formal worship service. Aside from the annual strawberry festival or harvest supper, we seldom went when I was little.

The family attitude toward church was illustrated by Dad's sarcastic remarks whenever someone he knew "got religion." In a mocking voice he would ask, "Are you saved? Did you get your sins forgiven? You better than us now, are you?" His hostile remarks pushed some people to the brink of tears, which made him laugh all the more.

This hostility toward everything church makes the story of my mother's conversion all the more amazing. I'm not sure what motivated her, but one day she decided to attend revival meetings at a small church in the neighboring village of Ginger Hill. Off she went night after night. When Dad gave her the "Are you saved" bit, she just spit back some emasculating comment, and it ended there.

The revival was led by a well-known guest evangelist. Every night the place was packed out with ninety to a hundred people stuffed into the sanctuary. Part of the fascination was the drama this preacher would bring to each night's service.

As people arrived, the song leader would lead the congregation in rousing gospel choruses and hymns. While everyone was singing, the evangelist was waiting backstage in makeup designed to make him look like Jesus. Wearing a white robe with blue sash, long dark hair, full beard, and sandals imported from the Holy Land, he looked like he'd walked straight off the set of *Ben-Hur*.

At just the right moment, this Jesus creature would mysteriously appear. He might poke his head out from behind a pillar, stand peering down upon the crowd from the choir loft, or look out from behind a curtain. Like an otherworldly apparition, he would show himself as though he were the Lord himself, and then quickly disappear.

Each sighting of the Jesus creature would incite loud shrieks and shouts from the congregation as the emotion in the sanctuary grew to fever pitch. People reached for the hem of his garment, sure that miracles would follow if they could only touch his robe. But imitation Jesus never let them get close enough. A few of the holiest would swoon back in their pews, evidence of heavenly power falling on them from above.

After Jesus slipped away, people would sing and clap all the louder, no doubt hoping that all this holy commotion would usher in the Second Coming. As the song service progressed, the evangelist would be busy backstage changing into his preacher clothes. Then, with perfect timing, he would walk out onto the platform and preach to a crowd of people as ecstatic as if they had witnessed the Resurrection itself.

When Mom told me I needed to join her one night, the thought sent me into spasms. Already terrified of God, I protested every way I knew how, even appealing to Dad for deliverance. One cross look from Mom, though, and I was headed to a come-to-Jesus meeting whether I liked it or not.

By the time we arrived, the church was packed, stifling hot, and short on fresh air. Claustrophobia kicked in, and I couldn't stop thinking of how I might escape.

Though the music sounded boring to my ears, I was fascinated with the spectacle, half church service and half vaudeville show. Many people looked like they were on the front end of a two-day drunk, singing loudly and swaying back and forth. I was surprised to recognize some in the crowd whom I'd seen stumbling out of Little Dicks Bar in Rankintown. Perhaps, like everyone else, they were hoping to escape damnation to the lake of fire.

Mom and I were sitting in the third pew on the left side of the church. About halfway through the songfest, I happened to look up at the closed door just left of the stage. The knob was turning ever so slowly. As the door began to creep open a fraction of an inch at a time, I could see a shadowy figure moving in the darkness. Chills went through me as if I had touched a bare electrical wire, and I almost passed out from fright.

There he was! Jesus, standing in the shadows, looking straight at me! He didn't look all that pleased to see me either. If I hadn't been trapped in my pew, I would have bolted from the church.

People started shouting and pointing at Hollywood Jesus. Contrary to what you learn in Sunday school, when Jesus came through the door this time, he didn't even knock. Folks began standing up, leaning over to get a glimpse, while others jumped out of their seats and ran over to our side of the church.

When I looked over again, he was gone. The believers went into a spiritual frenzy, shouting, "Hallelujah." Some cried; others sat back in their seats with their heads bowed in prayer. Me, I was just trying to breathe again, hoping no one would notice that I'd peed my pants a bit. When I looked at Mom, she seemed pleased I'd seen Jesus or, better yet, that he had seen me.

Made-up Jesus knocked the wind out of me and sent a crowd of people into the spiritual ethers, as if God himself had descended from heaven to goose a bunch of sinners off the road to hell and onto the narrow way leading to the pearly gates.

She Musta Been Born Again

One night of revival was more than enough for my half-crazed mind, but Mom kept going back night after night. Even Dad's taunting about "being saved" didn't faze her. Somehow the sideshow reached into her heart. The evangelist preached about being born again, and sometime during the two-week revival, my mother went to the altar and asked Jesus into her heart.

There may have been histrionics and more than a hint of manipulation wrapped into the nightly services, but God used imperfect people to advance his purpose. My mom ended up getting saved, and things started to change around our house. Not big changes, but small seeds that over time grew into important shifts in the way we did life. Some good. Others not so much.

The most notable transformation was that we began to attend church. Because of an argument that had occurred during the most recent strawberry festival—a derogatory comment from Dad about the berries—we didn't attend the Venetia Methodist Church but instead the Methodist church in the village of Gastonville, which, besides the church, was a speck of a place with a store, a post office, and an elementary school.

The Christianity we were exposed to was a mixed bag. The preacher was a fire-breathing man who believed in being born again. He was also anti–Roman Catholic. He would refer to the "Great Whore," which, of course, made a church service interesting to a teenage boy. Even so, the preacher had a genuine sense of the presence of God about him, which garnered a lot of respect.

Mom's newfound religious fervor translated into a form of discipleship that was a combination of evangelicalism and legalism with a hint of Pentecostalism. She wanted us to escape hell's fire by getting saved. At the same time she held the threat of temporal and eternal punishment over our heads in hopes of modifying our behavior.

What actually constituted sin was never all that clear. Bigotry and racism seemed to be okay, but drinking and smoking were not. Being kind was important unless the folks were Catholics or Italians. Forgiveness was extended for one's shortcomings unless a girl got pregnant before she was married. The rule of thumb was something like "Jesus loves you, but whatever you do don't get him angry!" Pretty much the same message we already understood about how to relate to Mom.

Girls and Church

One upside of becoming a churchgoer was Thursday night youth meeting. The small church had a vibrant group of teenagers, including several pretty girls. Some were my age; a few were already attending a local college. The college girls were especially interesting. Mentoring me in some of the more salacious facts of life seemed to be important to a couple of them. I felt blessed.

The leaders had a genuine love for Jesus and a deep concern for teenagers. They taught us about what it meant to be followers of Christ and encouraged us to get involved helping other folks. On Sunday afternoons they would take us to the area hospital to visit patients and sing a few hymns. Not really something that interested me, but I went along anyway. Did I mention the girls?

One aspect of youth group did freak me out. Every so often the leaders would hold special prayer sessions designed to get rid of any demons that might be afflicting teenagers, especially those struggling with sin. Those deliverance sessions, held in a small back room, would continue for hours, complete with wild emotional outbursts, kids saying they were hearing voices, and adults loudly commanding the spirits to leave.

For an anxiety-ridden teenager whose angry, unpredictable mother had already primed him to fear the impending judgment of God, the focus on demons left me playing on the edge of darkness. Why did I attend such meetings? Did I mention the older girls yet?

Lost and Found at the Syria Mosque

One day, the youth group leaders made an announcement—David Wilkerson, author of *The Cross and the Switchblade,* was coming to Pittsburgh's Syria Mosque, a 3,700-seat performance venue, and was bringing gang members from his ministry in New York City. Wilkerson was traveling the country speaking to youth about Jesus. The evangelist Kathryn Kuhlman was sponsoring the Pittsburgh meeting.

I knew nothing about Wilkerson and even less about Kathryn Kuhlman, but I decided I would go along for reasons already mentioned. So one Saturday afternoon, kids and adults from various local churches gathered in the parking lot of the local elementary school to board buses rented for the trip into Pittsburgh.

I was excited to make my way to the back of the bus and sit with a couple of the girls I knew. I was sure the ride would be fun and the trip back home in the dark even more so.

While we were settling in, one of the women from the church made her way back to where I was sitting. She told me she was glad

I'd decided to come along and then added, "There are a lot of us praying for you, Terry." The two girls giggled, and I stared at her, not sure what that meant. After an awkward pause she turned and walked back to the front. Meanwhile, I thought about how wonderful it felt to be sandwiched between two high school girls.

The ride into Pittsburgh took less than an hour. Because I'd rarely journeyed beyond our little town, it felt like an adventure. I was fascinated as we rode through the Liberty Tunnel and then across the Liberty Bridge. On the other side of the Monongahela River, we made our way into Oakland, passed the Cathedral of Learning on the campus of the University of Pittsburgh, and pulled up to the Syria Mosque.

I must have looked like a member of Ma and Pa Kettle's brood as I stood gaping at the tall buildings. Skyscrapers jammed close together, not a blade of grass between them, towering higher than anything I had ever seen. Cars and buses crowded the streets, one moment at a dead stop and the next moment racing past and belching exhaust into the polluted air. Hundreds of people were pushing through glass doors to get into the Syria Mosque.

Caught up in a great wave of people, I was swept through the doors, up the steps, and onto the first balcony. Luckily for me, a number of my friends had also landed there. Fighting my way across a crowded row, I sat down beside them. But because heights and crowded spaces always triggered my anxiety, the fun was already beginning to leach out of the experience.

It wasn't long before the music began. Hymns and gospel songs filled the arena. A middle-aged African American man sang a couple of solos, and at some point gang members with jet-black hair filed out and sat on the stage. People seemed pretty excited about that.

Then Kathryn Kuhlman floated onto the stage wearing a long dress with willowy sleeves that looked like angel wings. Looking out at the crowd, she asked, "Have you been waiting for me?" I hadn't been, but apparently a lot of other folks had. Suddenly the place went nuts. She laughed and extended her long arms while people applauded and the room turned electric.

Then she introduced Dave Wilkerson, who introduced some of the gang members who began to talk about what Jesus had done in their lives. I was especially taken by a guy named Nicky Cruz, who had some interesting things to say. It was *West Side Story* in living color.

By the time Dave Wilkerson began to preach, my anxiety was ramping up again. I couldn't wait for the whole thing to be done. I had no idea that things were about to get a lot worse. Wilkerson began to shout about sin and about how angry God was because of the whole deal. He started talking about the sword of the Lord cutting through the land, making it sound like God was about to mow down a lot of people. The picture of hell he painted had me feeling the flames.

There I was, in a rickety old wooden theater seat, squashed in on every side, high above the stage, in a balcony packed solid with people. Feeling trapped, I shifted my weight back and forth trying to restrain the impending storm. My mouth went dry, my palms felt clammy, and my breathing became rapid and shallow. Wilkerson was pressing every single one of my buttons.

He kept talking about God's judgment, waving his hands for emphasis, getting louder and louder. I couldn't stem the tide one more second. A full-blown panic attack exploded, and I had to get out of there. Jumping from my seat, I bumped knees and kicked shins all the way down the aisle. I was suffocating, and my heart was pounding out of my chest. A voice inside my head kept screaming that the sword of the Lord was coming to get me. It chased me down the steps and right out of the building.

Pacing back and forth in front of the Syria Mosque, I wanted nothing to do with Wilkerson, Kuhlman, or the freak show going on inside that building. I'd had enough. Just as I began to calm down, I was ambushed by another thought that propelled me into a second panic attack.

Here I was on the streets of downtown Pittsburgh. I had no idea where I was, didn't know where the bus was parked, and except for the kids I'd been sitting beside, I was clueless about where everyone else was seated. If I didn't find someone I knew before people started stampeding out those doors, I wouldn't know how to get home. Forget about being lost for eternity. There was a very good chance I would miss the bus.

Sweating profusely, I went back inside, planning to hang out in the men's restroom until I could return to my seat before everything ended. My friends and I would find the bus together. Any thought of sitting with pretty girls for the ride home was banished. I would have been glad to sit next to a warthog with cooties just to get out of there.

But there was one problem with my plan. The "sword of the Lord" wasn't just coming through the land, it had also invaded the men's john! The message was being piped in through speakers. Two things seemed obvious. First, I could run but not hide from God. Second, I couldn't escape Dave Wilkerson either!

Fleeing the restroom, I tried to catch my breath in the main lobby. After a few moments, I decided to make my way back to my seat. Once there, I tried blocking out the voice, but then I heard these words: "Do you want to go to hell? Do you want to spend eternity in the lake of fire? If not, I want you to get out of your seat, come down to this stage, and ask Jesus into your heart."

In a split second I knew the answer to both questions. I had already been in hell for the past hour, and I had no intention of spending eternity there. I jumped out of my seat as though I'd been catapulted from an aircraft carrier. Down the stairs I ran, heading for the stage. By the time I got there, the tension that had been building inside me translated into an ocean of tears. I knelt on the floor and cried my eyes out. A man came down from the stage and began to lead me through a prayer to accept the Lord.

After what I'd been going through, it was a great relief to let some of the emotion go. No doubt many of my tears were the overflow from an anxiety high. But it was more than that. Something happened deep inside me. I was touched by a force of love I had never known.

There, kneeling on that hardwood floor, with my nose running like the mighty Mississippi, I felt the hand of God reach into my soul. Something came alive inside me, and the only words that I had were that I was "born again." I knew that I had been forgiven by Jesus. More than that, I felt saved.

I stayed on my knees for some time. When I got up, I was shocked to see people from my church standing behind me, all smiles and tears. I was hugged and kissed all the way back to the school bus. Still blubbering as I walked onto the bus, I was taken aback as people applauded while I made my way to a seat toward the rear.

I had begun the trip to Pittsburgh excited for a chance to sit beside a pretty girl and maybe hold hands. If all went well, I might even nab a smooch or two on the way home, when no one else was looking. Instead, I sat in the last seat stupefied, stunned by a sucker punch from God that left me dazed and wondering what had happened.

I didn't question how genuine that moment kneeling in the Syria Mosque was. I was sure Jesus had entered my heart. More importantly I felt as though he had found a place in his heart for me. A seed of eternal life had been planted deep that night. I learned that Jesus was the answer to a question I hadn't been asking. What emerged into my teenage mind were new questions that produced more than a little anxiety. *What was this God really like?* Wilkerson's portrayal of wrath had run me into the streets sucking for air, and it was fear that had driven me to the stage.

But once there, I had an experience of God that was indescribably warm and accepting. *What should I do? Run from him as I always had, or say yes and come home to his embrace?* I was caught between comfort and condemnation, feeling a pull in opposite directions that would characterize my journey for years to come.

Five

BECOMING A WARDLE MAN

It was late when the phone rang. Mom picked up the receiver on the worn-out rotary telephone, answering it as usual with a shrill "Hello." Listening intently, she shook her head up and down as though the person who called could see her agreeing. After a few moments, she gave the telephone to my father.

Dad never seemed at ease with a phone in his hand. As soon as he started talking, his voice changed and he would begin speaking in short, jerky phrases. The first time he set up an answering machine, he cussed it nonstop. It wasn't until months later that someone told him his foul-mouthed tirade had recorded just fine.

That evening Dad took the receiver from Mom, answering with his usual "Yello," a contraction of "yeah hello." Listening silently for several moments, he hung up without saying a word. Then he turned and said, "Get your coats. We're goin' to Aunt Bess's."

Jumping up from our threadbare couch as if on assignment from God, Mom ordered us into the car. After climbing into our red-and-white DeSoto, with its push-button gearshift, we headed down the road to Rankintown. Since we rarely went out at night, this had to be serious. While he was driving, Dad whispered instructions to Mom to which she repeatedly nodded her head and said, "Okay."

When we pulled up to Aunt Bess and Uncle Harry's house, I saw several cars already parked in the long driveway. My cousin Jimmy crossed in front of our headlights and entered the house by way of the side door. Since neither Mom nor Dad explained what was going on, I tried to puzzle it out for myself. Maybe Uncle Harry or Aunt Bess was sick. Or perhaps they'd already died, or maybe a relative was about to be hauled off to jail.

As we walked through the door and into the kitchen, Evelyn and Aunt Bess were scurrying around with pots and pans, getting ready to cook something. I heard male voices coming from below. Dad quickly descended the steep stone steps into the basement, and the door closed, screeching like a red-tailed hawk.

As usual, I was told to sit with Uncle Harry in the living room. Since he was watching an episode of *Have Gun—Will Travel,* he wasn't in the mood to talk, which suited me fine. I was more interested in what was causing the buzz in the basement.

Things in the kitchen rattled on for some time before the basement door finally opened and Carrot popped his head out.

"Where's Terry?" he yelled.

Jumping up from the stuffed chair, I ran to the door.

"Get down here. We need you."

As many times as I had visited Aunt Bess and Uncle Harry, the basement had always been off limits. Now I was needed "down there." But for what? I began my descent into the depths of the "holy unknown," apprehensive about what might await me.

When the uneven stone steps threw me off balance, I grabbed for the old wooden railing. The smell of damp earth grew stronger as I descended the steep stairway. I could hear men's voices, the clang of tools, and my cousin Carrot spitting out instructions like Patton on a battlefield.

As I stepped onto the dirt floor, an unfamiliar odor assaulted me. Resisting the urge to cover my nose, I turned toward the back of the basement, then stopped in my tracks. The men were gathered under a large spotlight that was shining on something hanging from a dusty wooden beam supporting the floor above. I couldn't believe my eyes.

Carrot had gone out that evening and poached a deer from the neighbor's farm. Hunting was huge among my relatives, more religion than recreation. Caring about state wildlife regulations, not so much. To these men, there was no such thing as "in season" or "out of season," shooting hours, bag limits, or trespassing signs. The threat of arrest—and a few of them had been arrested—was never a deterrent.

I learned that Carrot and his son Jimmy had wrangled the deer through the kitchen and down the basement steps as stealthily as if they had been clandestine CIA operatives. Relatives had been secretly summoned to help butcher the deer and share in the bounty.

As I stepped closer, men were sharpening their knives, preparing to skin the animal and butcher the meat.

Carrot had decided this was the night I would join the company of men. Instructing me to take hold of the deer's back legs, he was going to teach me how to butcher a deer. Taking a firm grip, I glanced up at one of Dad's cousins, who shot me a big smile and said, "Attaboy, Terry. That's how you do it."

Even though I struggled with chronic anxiety, I was never squeamish. A few years before, an older cousin had handed me a paper bag as I was leaving his house, instructing me not to open it until I got home. As a joke, he had given me the leg of a deer he had bagged, severed at the knee with the hide still on.

What a gift! Secreting it in my closet, I would take it outside, make tracks along the ground and then imagine myself as Kit Carson tracking wild game across the Far West. I even named the appendage Rudy.

Before long poor old Rudy had become unbearably rank. It took Mom a while to figure out where the smell was coming from. She would come into my bedroom, complain that I hadn't taken a bath, and march me off to get clean. When her supersniffer discovered the real culprit, she burned it in the barrel in the backyard, and Rudy and I were forever separated. Things didn't go well for me, either, because Mom set my backside on fire with her hand and then told everyone how stupid I was to keep a deer leg in my closet.

But now here I was standing in Aunt Bess's basement. And this time everything was different. My cousin's "attaboy" was more than an affirmation. It was an invocation, the beginning litany of an initiation rite withheld from me until that one sublime moment. I had taken my first step away from the apron strings and into the circle of men. I was a squeaky voiced adolescent boy moving beyond the constraints of childhood into the sacred space where men wield mysterious powers. In the midst of cigarette smoke, the foul smell of entrails, and sweaty men cussing and drinking beer, I entered the shadowland revered by every boy I knew.

No longer relegated to the upstairs with the women and old Uncle Harry, I had entered a space in which men bragged, said bad words, sharpened long knives, and cut up poached deer in secret. This was my mountain-man rendezvous.

Though Dad paid no more attention to me than usual, other men seemed to notice me, playfully roughing me up, showing me how to skin a deer, and promising I would go hunting with them real soon. Covered in blood, I felt happier than I could remember. Nobody had to warn me to keep my mouth shut about the poaching. It felt great that they didn't have to tell me.

Soon after that, I joined Carrot and Jimmy on the first day of rabbit season. Dad went along, too, but seldom joined in after that. As I came of age, he quit going into the field, indifferent to hunting and even more indifferent to my desire to become a woodsman. But my cousins and uncles made up for it, mentoring me in what it meant to be a hunting man.

A Company of Men

The men in my life were marked by an uncultured masculinity. Dressed in worn-out work clothes, they rarely bothered to dig the dirt from beneath their nails. Ready for any challenge, they were good at fixing things and knew how to survive in the woods if they needed to. Some didn't shave regularly and others wore beards. Their hands were rough and calloused from professions like mining, farming, carpentry, and stoking the smelting furnaces down at the steel mill. Instead of expensive cologne, they exuded the fragrance of soil, tobacco, diesel fuel, and spirits. Blue-collar jobs and red necks were considered a badge of honor, part of our family crest.

Their speech was as colorful as they were, composed of a mixture of swear words, slaughtered English, and local slang. Cigarettes hung from the corners of their mouths, bobbing furiously as each man tried to outdo the rest with tales of bravado. Quarts of beer helped fuel their enthusiasm.

When it came to everyday conversation, "Jesus Christ" was a name often uttered, not out of piety, but because it served as an exclamation point rather than an acclamation of praise.

Most of the men were veterans. Three of my great-uncles had seen combat in World War I, while other relatives had served in World War II and Korea. Dad had been a drill instructor during the US occupation of Japan. After Uncle Frank finished his prison sentence, he did two tours in Vietnam. But no one talked much about their experiences. Dad said those who told stories usually hadn't been there. Even so, the effects of their wartime experiences leaked out in emotions and behaviors that haunted them for years and left marks on the rest of us too.

Despite the fact that so many of the men in my family had gone off to war, I never once heard any of them encourage their sons to join the military. Even Uncle Rob, who railed against draft dodgers during the Vietnam War, suggested I pack up and head to Canada as soon as I was old enough for the draft. I decided to go to college instead.

Regardless of all their flaws, which often made me uncomfortable, I loved being with Wardle men whenever they herded up in some grease-stained garage or overgrown backyard. These impromptu gatherings fueled by beer and cigarettes were to be my education and my entertainment. We were like redneck knights jousting for position in King Arthur's court, vying to see who could command the greatest respect.

Invariably the conversation turned to guns. One Saturday Dad took me along to Carrot's house for lunch before a rabbit hunt. The faded oak table was loaded with pots of coffee, homemade bread, and garden onions. Burt, Carrot's loud-mouthed neighbor, entered the back door carrying a brand-new double-barreled, 12-gauge shotgun, then passed it around the table like a new father sharing baby pictures. Each man held it reverently and then shouldered it for size. When my turn came, I put it to my shoulder but found my arms shaking under the weight, birthing more than a few snickers.

No one enjoyed guns more than Burt. He loved bragging about them. But his tune changed the day he dropped his pistol, shot himself in the foot, and shattered his pride. Burt had to settle for keeping a machete in his car after that because his wife had gathered up his guns and taken them to their son's house for safekeeping.

Cars were another favorite topic. The best were loud and fast.

Several of the men drove in stock-car races long after they should have retired. I spent countless hours watching engines being changed out, tested, and souped up before a big race.

Carrot bought a high-performance 1959 Chevy convertible that was so powerful he was afraid to drive it. But Dad loved driving it, especially with the top down. One Sunday afternoon, with Mom and me in the car, Dad pulled up to a stoplight on a four-lane stretch of road. Soon we were joined by a young guy in a hot rod who kept revving his engine, itching for a race. Right before the light turned green, Mom looked at Dad and said, "Get him!"

We laid rubber for a hundred yards, with Dad shifting through the gears like an Indianapolis 500 veteran. Since there were no seat belts, I held on for dear life in the back while Mom grabbed for the scarf she'd been wearing. Too late! It was gone with the wind. Passing the kid at over one hundred miles per hour, Dad didn't slow down until the hot rod wasn't even a speck on the horizon.

After a while, most of my cousins were driving their own fast cars, usually set up by their dads. My first car was a beater I bought during my second year of college.

The Wardle Thing

Years later, while attending a gathering of friends and family, my cousin Vic handed me some old family photos. As we looked at a picture of a distant cousin who'd been a great athlete, Vic remarked, "That guy could have made the pros had it not been for the 'Wardle thing.'" Noting the look of confusion on the face of a friend standing next to me, Vic gave a wry smile and simply said, "Women."

My grandfather was a case in point. He missed more work from carousing than illness and was forced into court more than once to face a paternity suit. Though Grandpap would head up to the mountains on deer-hunting trips, he never set foot in the woods because he was too busy with other kinds of adventures. I'm not sure how much time Dad spent in the woods either. I've always wondered whether he gave up hunting because he began feeling guilty about all the baggage that came along with that brand of hunting.

Whenever women or children weren't in hearing distance, the conversation sooner or later turned to sexual exploits, real or imagined. Issues of prowess were bragged about in the same way a millionaire might boast about his bank account.

I remember my first deer hunt. Tucked into a top bunk in a one-room cabin in the mountains, I listened as the men chewed the fat while playing cards. Assuming the younger guys had faded off, they began bragging about their sexual lives. All were married, yet each talked about unfaithfulness as though it were an accomplishment. They spoke about women with as much detail as they might speak about guns and cars.

It wasn't long before they began questioning the teenage men about their own experiences. The expectation was always clear. Real men get the women.

The idea of respecting women never seemed to cross their minds. Grandpap took a particularly utilitarian view of things, acting as though women had been created to serve his needs, whether that meant taking care of kids, cooking, cleaning, or satisfying his sexual appetite. Though he was brutal with my father, he was far harder on his daughters and stepdaughters.

Angry about a young man Aunt Peg had been dating, Grandpap once beat her so badly "she looked like she'd gone ten rounds with Joe Louis," as my dad described it. She stayed in bed for days, with a heart that may have felt more wounded than even her bruised and battered body. Instead of apologizing or being arrested for what he'd done to her, Grandpap simply took off on a three-day drunk. Sixty years later, my Aunt Peanut (real nickname) sat across the table from me and said, "I never saw your grandfather treat a single woman in our family with kindness. We all despised him."

A Seat at the Wardle Table

I couldn't throw a stone in our county without hitting a relative. Uncles and cousins were everywhere, or as Uncle Charlie once said, "Wardles are like dog crap after the snow melts. Piled up everywhere you look!" Despite the stinky comparison, it was great having a brotherhood that welcomed me into its company and that would stand by me when trouble came.

Their embrace pulled me away from the emotional storm that was my inner life. I loved how they would tell me to climb into their trucks when they saw me hitchhiking, invite me to the racetrack, or stop by to say hello. It didn't matter if they were half drunk or sober as judges. I was always glad to see them.

Sitting at the table of Wardle men meant that I could hunt their farms and join their gatherings. It also meant I had to respect them and share their values. I loved hunting and fishing, could salt my speech like the rest of them, and knew enough about cars to get by. As one of the only ones who played organized sports, I could steal the moment with a tale about the game we had just won. But some of their values didn't fit.

For one thing, they loved bravado. But I had so much fear. When night fell, it shouted at me just as loudly as it had in my childhood. I didn't dare open up about what I was experiencing because that would have meant surefire disqualification. No more place at the table for Terry.

There was also the matter of faith. At the time I was entering the world of men, I was also making baby steps as a Christian. This set up a huge clash of values. Another voice was calling me, one that made me feel uncomfortable about what I'd been hearing around the table of men. I didn't always pay attention to that voice, crossing the line when it suited me, bending a few rules, and getting into my share of fights—something that increased my stature among my male relatives. Knowing the disdain they had for guys who went to church, I hid my faith from them.

Things became especially uncomfortable whenever questions arose about whether I was "getting any." The language of sexual conquest was their native tongue, but I found it embarrassing and distasteful. Though "saving myself" was the furthest thing from my mind, I didn't see any reason to brag.

Once Uncle Carl took me aside to ask how far I was going with the girl I'd brought to dinner at his house. The grin on his face made me feel dirty. Though I wanted his approval, his expectations were challenged by something deep inside me that told me there had to be more to life than hunting trips, fast cars, fistfights, and sleeping around. Still, I wasn't ready to give up my seat at the Wardle table of men.

The tension between the world I had waited so long to enter and the new life I had tasted at the Wilkerson rally was not easily resolved. With one foot planted in each world, I lived a double life among two groups of people who didn't know each other. That decision pulled so hard in opposite directions that I didn't live fully in either. It wasn't long before my life was torn apart.

Six

DEVIL OR DISCIPLE?

It was a sweltering Friday, the summer before my senior year. Staying out all night with a group of friends I'd known since grade school seemed like the perfect antidote to boredom. Together we had concocted a lie we told our parents—that we were staying at a friend's house. Instead, we planned to find some up-all-night fun, like the time we "borrowed" a car to steal apples or when we were chased for sticking shotguns out the car window to shoot pheasants. The fact that it was hunting season didn't seem to matter to the authorities.

Determined to exorcise some darkness from tensions at home, I didn't think prayer was the way to get it done. I needed to run. In addition to the challenges that came from leading a double life, conflicts with Mom and Dad were escalating and things between them were even worse. I hated being at home, and they felt the same.

Tensions were at an all-time high in the country, too, with civil rights protests, the Vietnam War, assassinations, and riots breaking out in major cities. Several of my relatives voiced loud opinions about such issues, complete with detailed descriptions about what should happen to anyone who disagreed with them. Though I often disagreed, I knew enough to keep my mouth shut.

It didn't help that along with other announcements the high school principal would regularly read out the names of former students killed while fighting in Southeast Asia. That set a somber mood, especially since some of the dead boys had been friends and neighbors.

Whenever I thought about the future, I felt a churning in my gut. The draft loomed large, and college seemed out of reach given my academic performance. I had no idea what to do after high school.

My internal world was becoming increasingly chaotic. Though I fought hard to keep fear at bay, the strategies I chose were more destructive than the anxiety itself. Despite outward appearances, I was losing ground. To add to my insecurity, my steady girlfriend had just broken up with me, and I wasn't at all happy to part ways.

These were the conflicts that were boiling up inside me and around me that summer as we embarked on our night of adventure. Though the evening started slowly, it picked up steam after we scored some beer and got lit up.

"Hey, let's climb onto that flat roof above the clothing store," someone suggested. Grabbing fistfuls of gravel to throw at passing cars from an elevated height sounded like a great idea until two guys in a convertible pulled over to come after us. We leaped across the roof of an adjacent house, slid down the shingles to the gutter, and then dropped to the ground. Running like wildcats down the back alley, we didn't stop until we were well out of sight. Hiding behind the railway station, we shook with nervous laughter, happy we were still alive to tell the story.

By the time we came out of hiding, it was the middle of the night. With every store and bar closed down and our other friends long home, our scurrilous adventures threatened to end early. Then someone had a wonderful idea. *What about that guy who always loads newspapers into his car at 3:30 in the morning for delivery to neighboring towns? Wouldn't it be a blast to scare him?* The plan was to hide in the bushes and jump out of the dark when he left the house. As we pulled into his street, I had a flash of genius. My buddies would do the bushes prank, but I would crawl under his truck for the big surprise.

There were so many reasons why that was a bad idea. While the others crawled into the bushes, I scooted crossway beneath the truck with my head toward the driver's side. Right on time the door to his house opened and he walked to his vehicle. Just as he was reaching to unlock the driver's side, two things happened: my pals yelled from the bushes, and I stretched my arms from under the truck and grabbed his ankles.

Things got bad from there. Real bad. The guy started screaming like a man on fire, fighting the door handle to get into his truck. His horror sent me into a panic attack. I was terrified he was going to start the engine and run me over.

Like a snake on fire, I slithered out from beneath his vehicle as he hauled out of the cab, yelling profanities at the top of his lungs.

He was going to make us pay for what we'd done! Especially me! There may have been a little pushing and shoving involved, as I remember. I decided it might be good to not hang out in that part of town for a while.

God's Man

Thursday nights and Sunday mornings were my times to be with church folk. I went to youth group regularly, sang in the youth choir, participated in outings and activities, and traveled to perform and testify. I also attended the annual youth camp, rededicating myself to the Lord again . . . and again . . . and again. I had a Bible I read now and then and discovered that I slept better when I did. I didn't even mind the prayer meetings, as long as the demon thing was kept under wraps.

I also did a whole lot of repenting, both at youth group and at the altar on Sundays. Since guilt came easily to me, "laying my burdens down" became my specialty. Fearing God in the worst possible way, I tried hard to straighten up whenever he was around. When the opportunity came, I participated in service projects and performed good deeds to bank in my own treasury of merits.

Members of the church were nice to me, even patient. I must have seemed like a budding saint, halo yet to be earned. But the teenagers who attended youth group knew better. They were aware of my reputation at school and saw how I acted around my other friends. No doubt thinking it their Christian duty, they made sure the youth leaders knew about my wandering ways. It didn't help that

I had hurt their feelings by acting like I didn't know them apart from our time together at church.

One Sunday evening we were invited to sing and testify at a Pentecostal church in a small town across the river. I was anxious about such outings, fearing someone might know me and expose me for a hypocrite. The kids at this church were bused to our school, and I worried someone might call me out for making fun of them or pushing them around.

The congregation met in a house with a big sign on the roof that said, "Soul's Harbor," a fitting name for a building that was only a stone's throw from the Monongahela River. The low ceiling in the sanctuary was made of acoustic tiles lined with florescent lights. There was just enough space up front for a pulpit and kneeling rail.

The service began with high-powered gospel music accompanied by people swaying, arms waving, a liberal dose of spiritual "prayer language," and shouts of "Hallelujah" and "Praise the Lord!"

After being introduced as the visiting youth choir, we lined up two deep in the front of the church and sang several choruses with an occasional testimony interspersed. Responding with generous "amens" whenever a teen said a good word for the Lord, people seemed happy to see young people enthusiastic for Jesus. Filing back into our seats when we finished, we were satisfied we had shared the truth and shamed the devil.

Then the pastor—a middle-aged man who worked at the Clairton Steel Mill by day and served Jesus on nights and weekends—stood up to preach the evening message. Bible in one hand and handkerchief in the other, he was all in when he preached, pacing back and forth, stomping when the point demanded, getting low and rising up high to carry the message home to seeking hearts. His pace and tone reminded me of cars going around a racetrack—loud, then muffled, then loud again.

People loved the preaching and the preacher. I was caught up in the spirit of things myself, even considering a trip to the altar if the opportunity presented itself. I always had cleaning up to do whenever I went to church, and it seemed the Lord was open for business that night.

About the time I thought things were moving toward an invitation, the preacher stopped his sermon and looked out across the congregation. With a furrowed forehead and eyes squinted tight in a menacing stare, he surveyed the crowd as if hunting for someone who might have snuck in uninvited. The silence felt profound and unsettling. What happened next turned my butterflies into vultures and me into their meal.

"Young man, what is your name?"

He was looking in my direction. I was definitely in the line of fire. *Please, God,* I prayed, *let it be somebody standing behind me.* I would have been happy to duck in order to provide him with a straight shot at anyone but me.

"You. Right there. What is your name?"

With a stubby finger pointed straight at me, he took a couple of steps forward. As everyone turned to look, I stood frozen like a deer caught in headlights.

"Young man, tell me your name."

Just what I had feared—this was going to be payback time! I was sure God had told this pastor every bad thing I had ever done. One day people would speak of me like they did Sodom and Gomorrah, telling of fireballs launching from heaven and coming my way. There was so much heat building inside me that even my eyelids were sweating. Next to me someone kept nudging me in the ribs. "He wants to know your name. Tell him your name."

"T-Terry. Terry Wardle."

I spoke like a mouse about to die of starvation. When the pastor signaled that he couldn't hear me, someone stood up and shouted, "He said his name is Terry."

"Well, Terry, the Holy Ghost just told me something about you."

I knew it! I was about to turn to salt in front of the entire congregation. Mom had warned me about getting God mad. My face was about to roll straight up the aisle to the preacher's feet where he could heel stomp it like the head of a venomous snake.

"Son, the Holy Ghost has told me that you have an anointing on your life. God has laid his hand on you, young man. He has a plan for your life, Terry. Come on up here. We gotta pray for you."

People started standing, shouting, singing in the Spirit, stomping their feet, and praising the Lord. As a gentleman came over and took me by the arm to walk me up to the front, I looked over at the people I came with, some with tears in their eyes, others in stupefied jaw-dropping shock.

I must have looked like Bambi on ice as I made my way unsteadily forward. The pastor told me to kneel at the altar, helping me down with a firm shove on my shoulder. Then he called for the elders, who bolted from their seats like Seabiscuit exploding out of the gate. Within seconds the top of my head was covered with hands as men prayed down fire and prayed out sin.

Neither the power of the moment nor the weight of their hands on my head was lost on me. I was a seventeen-year-old kid suddenly dragged to the center ring with the Holy Ghost bearing down on him in front of all heaven and earth. Inside I argued with God like Moses at the burning bush, trying to hand off to someone else. But there was going to be no lateral that night.

I don't remember what they prayed. I only know their prayers were loud and filled with emotion. God was working, and there was no judgment, only power surging through me as though a warm stream of the Holy Spirit's love was cleansing my heart. I didn't want it to stop.

When I stood up, I knew something real had happened. Men clapped me on the back, and women hugged me with more affection than I'd ever felt, even on the best of dates. It was both embarrassing and exciting.

The pastor wasn't quite ready to let me go. "Young man," he said, "the Holy Ghost is calling you to be a man of God. Say yes, Terry. Say yes." But I was speechless.

That night, alone in my room and still spinning from the spiritual ambush that had knocked me to my knees, I made a promise to God. "Lord, I'm done with my sinful ways. I want to be a real disciple, like the ones in the Bible. I'm going to change; I'm going to witness. I'm going to be better from here out. I promise, God. I'm your guy."

One thing I knew. Things were going to change.

Help Me, Jesus

One day while I was busy mowing the lawn, a friend pulled his chopper into the driveway and then handed me a gift. "It's a treat for your weekend," he told me. After exchanging the acceptable version of a handshake: clasping hands, then thumbs, followed by hooking the tips of our fingers, off he went. Danny was a bona fide pothead who worked only enough to support his habit. I liked him. Looking around to ensure no one else was watching, I put the joint in my pocket for later.

That evening I went out with a buddy, taking my treat along to share. We found an out-of-the-way spot, lit up, and, unlike a well-known politician, inhaled deeply. After my friend took a few tokes, I finished the rest. Anticipating a sudden surge of hunger, we drove into the parking lot of the local Dairy Queen. That's when the lights went out. My lights, that is! The next thing I knew, a woman was yelling at me from behind the counter, extending an ice cream cone through the service window.

"Do you want this or not?"

I was in a fog so deep I didn't know where I was or what was happening. Taking the cone from her hand, I walked to the car and got in on the driver's side. Sitting motionless, I heard my friend repeatedly asking if everything was okay. Unable to reply, I threw the cone out the window only to discover that the window wasn't rolled down.

I began hallucinating, had trouble breathing, and went in and out of awareness. Things got even worse as I traveled beyond the borders of sanity. Before long I moved into full-blown paranoia, shouting that people were trying to kill me and that Dairy Queen had poisoned me with an ice cream cone I hadn't even eaten.

Until then, my friend had been experiencing a mellow high. But as soon as I started yelling, he began to have a secondhand freak-out. When I told him to take me to church, he drove my car into the parking lot and then promptly took off by foot.

The irrational fear that had been dammed up inside me for most of my life suddenly wanted out. Now it was magnified a hundred times. Sure that demons were after me, I wanted the pastor to chase them away. I walked up the steps to his front door and knocked hard. When his wife answered, she told me to wait right there. When she came back, she informed me that the pastor wouldn't see me. My pace, wording, and thousand-yard gaze must have tipped her off to my tripped-out state. Though I begged her to let me in, she shut the door, and I heard it lock behind her. I was lost.

The disciple Peter was told to forgive seventy-seven times, and apparently that night I reached my quota. I crossed a line of no return and experienced the pastor's version of being cast out to the place where people like me gnash their teeth. Whatever that meant. Adrenaline surged through me, and I started pacing back and forth, frantically repeating the phrase "help me." In a sudden moment of sanity, I remembered that my sister lived nearby so I walked to her house and beat on the door.

For the next thirty-six hours, Bonny used her best nursing skills to bring me down. By the time I crashed, I was exhausted. For a couple of days, I wondered if I would ever return. I felt like I was watching a slow-motion film through a dense fog, strangely disconnected from myself and my circumstances. It took days to get my feet under myself.

It turned out that the "treat" my friend had given me was called a killer joint, marijuana mixed with angel dust, also known as PCP, a drug used to tranquilize large animals like elephants and horses. Mixed with pot, it can induce hallucinations, rage, and extreme paranoia. In large doses, it can lead to seizures and even death.

A couple of days later, still too messed up to drive, I was hitchhiking on Route 88 when an old girlfriend, Cheryl Clark, picked me up. Instead of climbing in the front seat beside her, I crawled in the back and lay there holding my head. Cheryl asked if I was sick, and I told her about what had happened. She yelled for the remainder of the ride, telling me what a jerk I was and how much she hated me. At one point she stopped the car and told me to get out. I thought the bad trip had ended two days before. Apparently not.

Despite what had happened, I meant what I'd said after my encounter with God at Soul's Harbor Church. I wanted to be God's man. I was being pushed off course, not so much by peer pressure, but by the internal chaos of my never-ending dance with crazy. This wrestling match with darkness should have slapped me to sanity. Any conclusions I had come to about the whole thing . . . well, I didn't feel I had come to any. Except one.

"Don't smoke marijuana dusted with PCP."

Seven

COMING HOME

Geneva College had the distinction of being not only located in Joe Namath's hometown of Beaver Falls, Pennsylvania, but also the only school to accept my application. Despite dismal grades that trailed me through high school, I shocked everyone, especially myself, by performing well enough on the college entrance exam to be accepted by this small Christian college that prioritized science and the liberal arts.

In spite of my accomplishment and the "I'm cool" image I tried so hard to project, insecurity raged within me. It didn't help that Mom spent the drive to Beaver Falls injecting me with large doses of guilt and shame. Though I didn't realize it then, my leaving home had tapped into decades of ungrieved loss for her, which made her separation anxiety come out sideways.

My mother's not-so-tender goodbye consisted of commanding me not to embarrass her by screwing up. At that point, I felt like quitting before setting foot in a single classroom.

My mood was sour as she drove off. One look at the four freshmen and the apartment we'd been assigned to share, and I decided they were overprivileged know-it-alls, destined for a punch in the mouth. Though my assessment wasn't even remotely fair, I moved out as soon as I found a group of guys closer to my own tribe.

Those first few days and weeks of college were a complete culture shock. Students came from all over the world, with far wider experience of life and much greater academic savvy than I had. Guys sported long hair and beards, while the girls wore bell-bottom jeans and tie-dyed tops. In terms of cool, they seemed off the charts. One look at me and they must have wondered who was that rube who had slipped in when nobody was looking.

Though I felt intimidated and uncomfortable, I tried not to show it, adopting alternating strategies of either keeping my mouth shut or acting like I owned the place. Once in a while, whenever I stumbled over a word or slaughtered a common pronunciation, students would let a couple of chuckles leak out.

If the talk had been about hunting, fishing, or cars, I could have held my own, but engaging in conversations about what was going on in the world—current events that everyone else knew about—only made my head hurt. I had no idea who Abbie Hoffman or Joan Baez were, nor did I know where Kent State was located or the meaning of *antidisestablishmentarianism.*

Despite my rough and uncultured ways, I managed to make

friends with students I thought might tether me more tightly to my anemic faith. One friend suggested I try out for the soccer team, and I ended up being a four-year starter. But because I'd brought more baggage from home than the suitcases I'd unpacked in my room, there was a lot they had to put up with, like my foul mouth and rebellious ways. For some reason, they stuck with me.

When it came to my soccer games, mine were the only parents who never showed up, not that I expected them to. Though part of me didn't want them there, another part felt stung by their absence. During the four years I played on Geneva's team, not once did I look to the stands to see them cheering me on. Other families came and even dragged me along for dinner afterward, but my folks never made it.

I knew Mom had a hard time when I left for college, but Dad didn't even blink. He'd been so emotionally hammered by Grandpap's treatment of him that he didn't have much to give me.

Though my college career began with a brief season of religious zeal, it wasn't long until I stopped going to church. As I settled into campus life, familiar patterns reasserted themselves until my lifestyle began to match the way I had always lived. Even though I reverted to form, I was glad my Christian friends still wanted to hang out with me. There was something about them—a sense of deep peace and contentment—that I wanted for myself. I just didn't know how to get it.

Despite the fact that I kept trying to change, it seemed I couldn't. It wasn't just that I wanted to cross the line of good behavior. It seemed I *had* to. Acting out was the only way I knew to silence the screaming emotions that chased me around day and night.

Anger Management

Instead of things settling down as college progressed, things got worse and I became increasingly angry, getting into arguments at a moment's notice. I dusted it up on the practice field and got thrown out of a soccer game for threatening a referee over what I saw as a bad call. My irritability was such a constant that one of my best friends told me he hated hanging out with me. Still he stuck by me.

I had hoped that prayer would bring some peace to the storm in my guts but found that marijuana did it quicker. Given my lifestyle, it was remarkable I never got kicked out of school. At the time I thought I was putting up a good enough front to fool school authorities. But now I realize they were simply extending grace to a mixed-up college kid.

At the beginning of my sophomore year, I began dating an attractive girl who touched a place inside that longed for intimacy. Before long we fell in love, but Jesus was most certainly not the center of that relationship. She once told me that some holier-than-thou type told her we couldn't be in love because we weren't Christians. I made my way to his room to convince him he was wrong. I may have proved his point.

During our senior year my girlfriend and I became engaged. Though Mom and Dad were fine with the news, her parents were opposed to the marriage. She came from a high-dollar clan located in the ritzy part of Pittsburgh. No doubt her family was embarrassed by the thought of a son-in-law with a white-trash pedigree who would never be rich enough to support their daughter in the style to which she had become accustomed. Their voices blended with the crowd of other voices in my head that were constantly reminding me I wasn't enough. More fuel for the fires of my self-contempt.

No matter the source, whether a blue-collar beat down, an academic meltdown, or a high-society putdown, being me always fell short. Near the end of my senior year, I was ready to either run away or light a fire and burn everything down.

By the time my last semester rolled around, my girlfriend had already graduated and moved home to accept a teaching job in Pittsburgh. My plan was to finish school and then find a decent job. As soon as that happened, we'd start building a life together.

As the semester progressed, I became increasingly toxic. So much so that many of my closest friends began to avoid me. Those who didn't, I pushed away. Most nights I ate alone in the dining hall. Even playing soccer was stressful because I couldn't stop arguing with other members of the team. In terms of my remaining classes, I did the bare minimum to squeak by. I hated everything—the school, my prospects, everybody around me. I especially despised myself. My feelings regarding faith were about the same.

Worst Day

I'd had a lot of bad days during my time in college, but the worst of them started after a team loss that I probably caused. By evening, I was raging, so desperate that I wanted to hurt someone, knowing I was the most worthy candidate. The night started by my going out on my fiancée and hooking up with a freshman from my speech class. After dropping her off at her dorm, I drove my beat-up car behind the field house, sat in the front seat alone, and got high.

When I pulled into the parking lot of my apartment building, I met up with a couple of guys looking for something to do. The best idea they could come up with was to try to track down a guy by the name of Raymond Robinson. Called Charlie No Face or the Green Man, he was something of an urban legend. People said his face had practically melted away from an electrical accident when he was a nine-year-old boy.

People also said the Green Man came out only at night, spending his time walking along a lonely road because he didn't want people to see his face. I knew where he lived, so we headed out to see if we could find him. Turning a bend in the road close to his house, we spotted a figure in the headlights.

As we slowed down and pulled alongside him, Charlie No Face turned away, standing motionless up against the bank. As I rolled down the window, one of the other guys called out his name, offering him some cigarettes, which I handed him through the window. This wasn't a gesture of kindness on our part. We simply wanted to lure him close to the car so we could get a good look at his disfigured face. We were no different than all the heartless people who paid their dime to ogle circus freaks. In this case the price of admission was a pack of Winstons.

After completing our twisted errand, we headed to a local bar for steak sandwiches and beer and then headed home. Since my roommates were gone for the weekend, I returned to an empty apartment.

Throwing myself on the bed, I lay still as shame rushed over me.

Everything I had done that evening was ugly. I could smell the stench of it on my clothes. A profound sense of meaninglessness settled over me. No one had to tell me I was lost. I felt it marrow deep.

Hopelessness descended like a steel blanket, suffocating whatever life I had left. It wasn't guilt that had me by the throat—though I was guilty—but a sense of complete emptiness. I had looked into my soul and discovered there was nothing there but an endless black hole.

I wept. Then I tried to pray. But nothing came. Hadn't I been down that road so many times before? What was the use of uttering words as empty as my soul? Why should I bother? The scripture that came to mind and seemed to fit was the one about a dog returning to its own vomit. Over and over, I had stepped away from the Lord and now I was reaping the consequences. I deserved whatever was coming my way. God was good, I was not. That much was clear.

There was too much pain. Pain from other people's choices, pain from my choices, and the excruciating pain I had caused others. I had landed in a place I never intended—in the belly of the whale with no way out. Somewhere deeper than my despair a voice cried out begging for change.

I searched my mind for a word or thought that might bring a sliver of light. But there was nothing. Then an obscure Scripture passage poked its head out of the hole I was in. It was about hating the clothes stained by sin. It's all I had, so I thought, *Why not?* After stripping off my clothing, I stuffed everything I'd been wearing into a paper bag, took a shower, and then went to bed. But as I lay there in the dark, I realized it wasn't enough. Pulling on a fresh pair of jeans and a clean T-shirt, I got out of bed and headed to the backyard clutching the bag of dirty clothes.

I placed the bag near a filthy garbage dumpster, took out my lighter, and set it on fire. Watching my private bonfire light up the night, I stayed until the flames died down, then stamped out the burning embers until only the ashes remained.

Best Day

Raising my head and looking at the sky, I said, "The only way I will ever do what I did tonight will be if I am wearing those clothes." I made that promise to myself and no one else. I meant every word.

Determined to find a way home to the heart of God, I walked down the empty road that led toward campus. It was two in the morning, in the middle of a night as dark and cold as my heart.

With no destination in mind, I simply kept walking. I wanted to scream from all the shame I was feeling. When I rounded the corner near Sparky's Pizza Shop, it hit me. Above the shop was an apartment where some Christian guys lived. I climbed the outside steps, then reached out and beat loudly on the door. When one of them opened it wide enough to see who was there, he stared at me as though the devil himself were staring back at him. A couple of others entered the hallway behind him, wondering what the fuss was about.

"What are you doing here?"

"I need some help. I guess I kinda just found myself here and felt like I was supposed to ask you guys for help."

"What kind of help?"

I hesitated. I hardly knew what to say.

"I want to rededicate my life to Christ. I want you to pray with me."

One of the other guys mumbled, "Oh brother!" and turned to walk away. Another stopped him. "No, wait, I think he means it."

For the next hour, I knelt on the hardwood floor of their apartment and cried my heart out. I was blubbering like a baby in front of guys I barely knew. Years of pain and disappointment pushed to the surface determined to get out. It was impossible for me to hold myself together. I was broken. In the midst of a flood of prayers and tears, that shabby living room became a sanctuary, its beat-up coffee table an altar where I rested my head as I confessed the terrible things I had done that night.

Twenty-four hours earlier, I would never have knocked on their door. Had they approached me, I would have ignored them or pushed them away. Now I wanted them close. In fact, they couldn't get close enough. There was something familiar about what was happening. Men's hands resting on my head and shoulders, their voices ascending to God as they interceded for me. As hope slowly surged, I sensed something moving deep inside me. I couldn't describe what was happening, but the word *deliverance* crossed my mind.

Unlike earlier episodes of prayer, I made no promises about being different. I knew that was beyond my power. I just cried and repeated a small prayer I had been taught one night in youth group: "Jesus, Son of David, have mercy on me a sinner."

Years earlier, the best day of my life, the one I'd spent slipping and sliding through the mud with a friend, had suddenly turned into my worst day, leaving me in emotional pain that never went away.

In that small apartment above Sparky's Pizza Shop, I experienced the grand reversal. I gave my bondage to the Lord, and he gave me freedom in return. Instead of mourning, I was comforted; shame was traded for joy; and ashes were exchanged for beauty. It all sounded so biblical.

In a short space of time, my worst day had turned into my best day.

For so many years I'd been splashing around in the shallow end of the pool. Though I'd asked the Savior into my heart, I had never gotten on my knees to declare him Lord of my life. Though the time had come to move beyond my childish faith and step into a grown-up journey toward wholeness, I was only beginning to understand what that might mean.

Above that little restaurant, in a ratty apartment that should have been condemned years ago, I discovered the startling truth: I was not condemned but loved. Though I didn't even know their names, the guys who lived there were like brothers helping me to answer a question that had been posed to me years earlier in a small church just a stone's throw from the Monongahela.

Yes, I wanted to be God's man. Radical changes were coming, and some would be costly. I knew that. But I felt hopeful that if I followed him, Jesus would be there for me, leading me on the journey. He would show me where to begin and then give me the strength to walk it out.

The mess inside me still needed to be untangled. What had built up over many years would take a long time to resolve. But killing the pain my way hadn't worked. It had only brought despair. It was time to try a better way.

I used to wonder why the Bible identifies some people by the worst thing about them. Like the Gadarene demoniac, Blind Bartimaeus, Simon the Leper, or the woman caught in adultery. Why commemorate them by calling to mind something negative when each had been healed, when each had been transformed?

But now I got it. Jesus found them on their worst days and then changed their lives. I understood. Worst day, best day.

Eight

"SISSY BOY"

As I pulled into my parents' driveway, I found myself searching for the perfect words to deliver news about my future I knew they wouldn't want to hear. Entering through the garage and trudging up the basement steps, my heart felt like it was about to jump out of my throat. I wondered if this was how my sixteen-year-old cousin had felt the day she told her parents she was pregnant.

I had graduated from college straight into a recession. Gas lines were everywhere, and good jobs were impossible to find. Instead of opening the door to a promising career, my shiny new bachelor's degree earned me a minimum-wage job at the Allied Chemical plant in New Eagle. Despite the impressive-sounding corporate name, the company's mission was to manufacture mothballs as well as deodorizers designed to fasten onto toilets with a metal hook. My grunt-level job involved mixing solutions for the deodorizers and handling large amounts of naphthalene, which meant that I smelled like a mothball most of the time. Those three months at Allied Chemical were anything but a waste because that's where God began speaking to me about my future.

When I walked into the living room, Dad was half asleep on the flowered couch, blowing puffs of air through his lips. Mom was working a crossword puzzle while sitting in the stuffed chair next to the picture window that faced Grandma's house. Putting down her paper, she greeted me with "Oh, you're here. I thought you were working today."

Dad simply grunted "Hi," shifted the pillow under his head, and then turned on his side facing the back of the couch.

I wasn't too worried about how Mom would take the news. Even though her faith could be rigid, I knew it was real. She'd been attending church faithfully ever since that crazy revival and had even started teaching a Sunday school class. Still, I couldn't imagine she would be pleased with the news I was about to share.

Without easing into the topic, I told my parents about my plans: "I've decided what I am going to do with my future. I'm starting seminary next fall so that I can become a pastor."

There, the words were out, and there was no turning back. I had just jumped off a cliff, and in a few moments I'd know whether I'd landed on the rocks or in the water.

Turning her head slightly to one side, Mom tried to take in what I was saying. Though she looked surprised, she didn't seem angry or disappointed. "Are you sure?" she asked. "You don't know anything about preaching religion or that kind of stuff. That wasn't in your schooling, was it?"

"That's what seminary is for," I assured her. "I'll learn all that. I know this is what I'm supposed to do, and I've made up my mind. I've been accepted and have a full scholarship for my first year. It's a school in Pittsburgh."

What came next shocked me. A gentle smile spread across Mom's face as she spoke. "Well, we may not understand all this kind of thing. But if that's what you believe you're supposed to do, your dad and I will support you."

Support me? Really? Had Jesus just paid a visit to my parents in the middle of the night and talked to them about what I was going to do? Were these my folks?

I felt stunned. If ever I believed that prayer changed things, that moment sealed the deal. I let out a deep breath and lifted up a silent prayer: *Thank you, Jesus. This is unreal.*

Dad hadn't said a thing yet, not that I expected him to. Mom had ripped into him so often over the years that he usually kept his mouth shut. Sometimes he would blow up about an issue, but it didn't happen that often. When it did, he'd come unglued, kick the dog's food bowl up in the air, spit out some well-chosen words, and then sit down in his easy chair to watch television like nothing had happened.

I knew my father wouldn't be happy about my decision, but I began to hope that Mom's attitude would push him across the line so that he could at least offer grudging approval. These days Dad and I didn't see eye to eye about much. He kept warning me not to hang around his friends because "they hate hippies with long hair." Since he was embarrassed by my shoulder-length hair, I was sure he felt the same about me. After four years of college, I no longer saw the world through his eyes. Since he'd quit hunting and fishing years before, there was nowhere we could connect.

Just as I was starting to relax, Dad roused himself. Standing up from the couch, he looked straight at me. I had seen that look before and was sure dog food was about to drip from the ceiling. Tensing up, he started breathing heavily and then said, "What a waste! Why don't you get a real job and work for a living?"

Then he turned and walked out of the house.

I knew Dad had chosen his words with care, communicating maximum disdain for the decision I'd made. What he didn't say outright, but what I had suspected for years, was now plain to see. He thought his son was a sissy boy.

Gone Soft

I should have seen it coming. For many of the men I knew, the only thing lower than a church-going man was a preacher. To them pastors were an effeminate mixed breed, more given to tea parties than hard work. Instead of respecting men in ministry, they made a blood sport out of embarrassing them, asking questions about a car engine or rifle caliber for hunting deer that were designed to reveal how soft they were.

I remember standing next to a cousin at my grandmother's interment when a pastor asked if he could pray for him. "Don't you try to shove Jesus down my throat," my cousin spat back, "or I'll pour beer down yours." At the same service my uncle walked away from the graveside grumbling about the fact that the pastor had talked about

Grandma going to heaven. "Who wants to go to heaven?" he remarked to a couple of gravediggers who were standing nearby. "All the beer and women will be in hell, so that's where I plan to go." They all had a good laugh over that one.

I knew my decision to enter the ministry would change the way a lot of the men in my family viewed me. Though some accepted my choice despite feeling puzzled by it, many others did not. As these relationships chilled, I could sense their unease whenever I came around.

One time I went hunting with some of my old pals. As we reached the edge of private property, a relative told me to take my orange vest off so we wouldn't get caught hunting posted land. When I told him I wasn't going to hunt on someone else's property, he said, "Watch out, preacher, your mangina's showing," a derogatory put-down spit out like venom to shame men perceived as weak and effeminate. There was something about being a pastor and emasculation that seemed to go together for those guys.

A couple of them threatened to show up the first day I preached, sit in the front row naked, and then tell everyone all the bad stuff I had ever done. I knew they were joking; at least I hoped they were. That wasn't what bothered me. But it hurt to see their disrespect for something so important to me.

Many of the men in our community—relatives and family friends—had invested in me when Dad didn't have time. They had welcomed me into the circle, taught me about the woods, and treated me like an important part of the tribe. They had initiated me into manhood, and now it seemed they were revoking my membership.

I had always suspected that Dad was annoyed by the fear I struggled with as a kid. More than a few times, people told me about demeaning comments he had made behind my back. Though every remark hurt me, deep inside I secretly harbored some of the same opinions about myself.

When he told me to "get a real job," his comment cut deep. Wardle men tolerated so many things—drinking, breaking the law, immorality, and even dynamiting a neighbor's house. But being weak wasn't on their list. I had broken the man code. Becoming a pastor meant I was a waste, that I had chosen a job that didn't demand hard work. It was a public declaration that I was soft.

Dad's response had tapped into an unhealed wound I had carried since boyhood. Some dark power knew right where to poke and whose finger would hurt most. If there was any good news in the encounters with Dad and other members of the family, it was that my emotional low didn't send me back to an old path. That alone was grace.

By then my girlfriend and I were still together, but she flipped when I announced my plans to go to seminary. We'd been a couple for two and a half years and had set plans in motion for our marriage. I'd been saving up for a ring, and we'd both been eager to build a future together. Before that night at Sparky's Pizza, there was little to make her think I took being a Christian seriously. After that, she must have hoped I was going through a phase that would soon be over or that she could use her charms to woo me back across the line. But I wanted her to join in my transformation. Asking her to attend church with me didn't go down well in the slightest.

When I disclosed my plans about seminary, she called me a few names and told me to leave. She wanted nothing to do with someone "into religion." I walked out and never saw her again. Though I didn't blame her and though I still cared about her, I knew that given my history I had to make drastic decisions about how I was going to live.

The pain from these changes went deep. But I hoped it was the short-term pain necessary for me to experience long-term gain.

It didn't feel like gain, however. If the Lord was pruning me for better days, it seemed he had grabbed a chainsaw with a dull blade. A lot of blood got spilled on the ground in those early days, and it seemed like much of it was mine.

Saying yes to God made me feel like I was being pulled through a knothole backward. I had scrapes on the backs of my ears to prove it.

It wasn't as though the Lord provided a blueprint for how I should respond to him. The only thing that made sense to me was to ruthlessly show up where he seemed present and to run away from anywhere I thought he might not be. It was difficult to know how much of my newfound fervor was Spirit driven and how much was just gutting it out and doing the right thing. One thing I knew for certain: I had seen the darkness and had no intention of going back there. Nor did I ever want to do anything that would demand a second bonfire of the undies!

"Sometimes I Thank God . . ."

Before starting seminary, I devoured books I thought might help me and even preached a couple of times at a small country church.

Fortunately no pew streakers ever showed up. Though I worried about my delivery, no one else seemed concerned.

It took a while for members of my home church to begin to trust the changes in me. My double-minded life had given them whiplash far too many times. But I never again did drugs, went drinking, or slept with a girl until I got married.

Despite the rejection I felt, I continued to move forward. It wasn't a happily-ever-after scenario because there were still so many unhealed wounds. But good things started falling into place, and doors began to open.

One day, an old buddy from the neighborhood stopped by to talk. Always up on the latest gossip, he threw out a new tidbit. "Hey, did you hear that Cheryl Clark cut off her engagement?"

I jumped up so fast I almost left my skin on the chair. Without taking a breath I shouted, "I'm going to marry her!" I yelled so loudly that Mom ran into the room to see what was going on while my buddy looked at me like I was nuts.

Cheryl had been my high school girlfriend. She was also the girl who had picked me up in the middle of my bad drug trip and then kicked me out of the car. Beautiful, free, and now a follower of Christ, she seemed like everything I longed for in a wife. It had been a little more than six months since my previous girlfriend and I broke up. I had promised God I wouldn't date until the right one came along. Cheryl was the right one for me. I knew it.

Unfortunately, Cheryl didn't know it, nor did she warm to the idea of getting back together after so many years. Neither did her father or mother. My reputation as a "bad boy" had grown so large that they wanted to keep me as far away from their daughter as possible. But I wasn't about to give up. Time and persistence eventually won the day, and she finally agreed to marry me. I'll never forget the night I arrived to ask Cheryl's father for his blessing. When he strapped on his revolver, I told myself he was joking. Odd, though, that no one was laughing.

After a beautiful wedding, we lived through one of the roughest first years on record. Between seminary, work, preaching at a small church on Sundays, and having a baby eleven months after our wedding, the whole thing threatened to burn us to the ground. And then there was the unaddressed wounding thing.

We learned fast that accepting Christ doesn't heal everything. There was more than a little toxic waste in both our lives, which made things rough between us. Unrepaired emotional ruptures, especially from my past, created more problems than human love and affection could fix.

When the unprocessed pain from the past raised its ugly head, it stole many possibilities, in some cases robbing us of hope. We ended up bouncing off one another, fighting for solutions in our marriage that couldn't be found until we attended to personal wounds from the past. It took years before we understood that.

Step by step, with prayer and determination, we were able to gut out the hard times and build a family and a ministry. Even though our relationship ended up in the ditch from time to time, we managed to stay together, motivated by our dedication to the Lord and to our three children.

My relationship with Mom and Dad also improved. Because of

the family no-talk rule, we never discussed the past. That was off limits. But Dad began to accept the idea that a person could be a pastor and not be soft. That seemed like a Jesus-walking-on-water kind of miracle to me. My parents also adored our children, proving to be far better grandparents than parents.

Ministry was flourishing as well, and that was a big surprise. Though I was raw theologically and had more passion than wisdom, a lot of people came to Christ through my preaching. I began to get opportunities to speak in other churches and was tapped to lead some denominational programs. Invited to serve as a keynote speaker at a large conference in Orlando, I was thrilled, especially when other pastors congratulated me. It felt great when my gifts were applauded. Finally, I was a somebody, a man making his mark.

Entering the ministry had meant losing my seat at the Wardle table. My place at that table was secure only if I met certain requirements. When I stopped drinking, doing drugs, carousing, and acting out, I lost my place. Painful as it was to leave behind so many close relationships, God gave me the strength to move forward.

What I didn't realize was that finding success in ministry earned me a seat at the table again. I thought it was a different table, but it wasn't. I had traded the Wardle code for a religious code that valued performance and giftedness. Measuring up was still the name of the game. It would take many years and a lot of pain before I would realize that old wounds always found new ways to keep me in bondage.

Nine

FALLING DOWN THE LADDER OF SUCCESS

"Terry, we'd like to see you in the trustee board room in thirty minutes."

While standing on the sidelines enjoying a soccer game at Nyack College, I had just been summoned to the biannual meeting of the board of trustees for the college and its denominational seminary. The surprise summons didn't bode well.

After serving in pastoral ministry for more than a decade, I had accepted a faculty appointment at Alliance Theological Seminary in New York two years earlier. Despite how well my previous ministry had gone, my years as a pastor had been marked by a nightmare—a classic recurring anxiety dream. It began with me standing behind a pulpit, looking out at a large crowd. As everyone waited for me to begin speaking, I was frantically searching for my notes. Sensing the restlessness in the room, I stepped out from behind the pulpit to explain the delay, only to be met by expressions of surprise. Glancing down at my shoes, I realized I had forgotten to put my pants on! Afterward, I would awaken to a profound sense of inadequacy, followed by relief when I realized it had been only a dream.

Teaching at the seminary did nothing to improve my sense of relief because now the nightmare had morphed into reality. I wondered how long it would be until others began to realize my rear end was hanging out for everyone to see. I felt like a faintly flickering night-light, compared to my colleagues, whose brilliance shone like floodlights.

At my first chapel service, I sat between two of my new colleagues. Realizing I had forgotten my Bible, each offered to share his with me when it was time for the Scripture reading. *A nice gesture,* I thought, until I realized that both were reading not from an English translation but from the original Greek text! I didn't even know the Greek alphabet. I don't remember a word of the sermon because I was too busy invoking Dorothy's mantra from the *Wizard of Oz:* "There's no place like home. There's no place like home." In other words, *Get me outa here right now!* But without a pair of ruby slippers to help me relocate, I was trapped like a mule between two Thoroughbreds.

It didn't help that the professor who had held my position before me was a Christian superstar by the name of Ravi Zacharias. Ravi was already beloved globally and adored locally. Students traveled far and wide to study under him and spoke in almost hushed tones whenever his name was mentioned. And then Ravi left the seminary, and I came to take his place.

While Ravi was a world traveler, I had barely traveled outside my hometown. Though I had some local impact, beyond the second road past the post office, I was pretty much an unknown. Instead of increasing my stature, most of the guys I had rubbed shoulders with had left grease stains on my clothes. Not even a big fish in a small pond. I had been more like a minnow in a bathtub. At least that's how I saw it.

The first two years at the seminary were a stretch. What saved the experience was that I loved the students. Many of them, not much younger than I, camped out at my house and loved on my family, extending a lot of grace to a young professor.

After a while I developed some ancillary programs that grew in popularity. I also spent a lot of time with students doing ministry in New York City, which forced me out of my comfort zone and expanded my heart for people from other cultures. My first two years as a seminary educator proved to be the greatest education I ever had.

As time wore on, lingering anxieties began to wane, and I felt like I was doing precisely what I had been created to do. A sense of peace and contentment began to settle in and grow. Unhealed wounds were still there, but they were sound asleep.

If only things had stayed that way.

Too Wounded to Say No

After receiving the summons to the trustee meeting, I hurried home, changed into a suit, and made it to the meeting on time. The long wooden conference table surrounded by an impressive array of well-known businessmen, pastors, physicians, and other respected leaders did nothing to calm my jitters. Then the board began to question me on a wide range of topics related to seminary education.

Certain the jig was up, I braced myself, thinking I was about to receive a formal rebuke for posing as a professor. But as the questions kept coming, the truth slowly dawned on me. The board hadn't summoned me to render judgment on my poor performance but to interview me for the seminary's top job, a position I hadn't even applied for! In most other institutions, the post of executive director would have been called the presidency.

I had barely made it home before the telephone rang. On the other end of the line was the president of the board, and he was offering me the job plus a huge raise in pay. I couldn't call it a dream come true because I had never had the audacity to imagine an opportunity like this.

What a shock! Terry Wardle, from Coal Dust, U.S.A., was being offered the dual position of chief executive officer of Alliance Theological Seminary and vice president of Nyack College. Alliance was a major seminary with campuses in New York and Puerto Rico. How was it possible the board wanted me to become the new leader? This was the greatest affirmation I had ever received, and I was far too wounded to say no.

Being asked to sit at the big boys' table felt great. The local newspaper ran a story, and the denominational magazine did a full write-up about my family, complete with photos. I had been promoted to the front row, and the view was incredible. With an expense account, an executive office, a personal assistant, a secretary, and access to movers and shakers who hadn't previously known my name, I found that doors began to open. Before long I landed my first book contract and was speaking across the country.

Though I didn't realize it, I had just taken my first big step down the ladder of success.

Despite the acclaim, something inside kept telling me this new position wasn't right for me. But I wouldn't listen. Instead, I embraced it as a sacred trust and a sign of God's kindness. Being a good steward was important. I wanted to please God by doing a good job, proving to those who'd chosen me that they hadn't made a mistake. But that didn't keep me from being scared out of my mind.

Hard work paid dividends and yielded several early successes. But there were signs that all was not well. Displeased by my appointment, the old guard began to rear up. Rallying support, they flooded board members with letters and telephone calls expressing their opposition. They had three beefs. First, they said I was too new to the denomination. Second, they thought I, at thirty-four, was too young for the responsibility. Third, they took issue with me on theological positions that varied from those held by their tradition. Their gripes were on target, and had I been a more secure man, I would have understood this and turned down the position when it was first offered. But I wasn't, so I didn't.

Things got ugly fast. One day, someone handed me a collection of written protests, a few of which were brutal. "People like Terry Wardle eventually abandon the faith or become psychopaths," one read. "I will rejoice when I see his ministry in ashes," another stated. And then, my personal favorite: "Terry Wardle is like a piece of apple pie with dead flies mixed into the savory cinnamon." Nasty as they were, these relentless personal attacks had hit the bull's-eye of my own chronic insecurity. I was crushed.

It wasn't just a thirty-four-year-old man they were hitting. Without knowing it, my attackers were assaulting a small boy who was still trapped in an emotional firestorm caused years before by unhealed trauma. A healthy person would have found the situation challenging. But to an unhealed man like myself, it was devastating.

Members of the board started backing away in order to get out of the line of fire. Their lack of support added to my inner turmoil, which started leaking out in troubling ways. Before long I was battling generalized anxiety, finding it hard to sleep at night, and feeling claustrophobic whenever I was on an airplane or in the back seat of a car. Tensions built up at home, causing a serious rift between Cheryl and me.

Not knowing what else to do, I spent long hours praying, reciting the adage "Glance at your problems but gaze at God." That's usually great advice, but I was operating in such a thick fog that I couldn't manage to catch a glimpse of the Lord.

Though I tried hard to project an appearance of strength and resolve, inside I was a mess. Unaware that the real problem lay in the past, I kept fighting what was in front of me. Finally, after two years of near emotional exhaustion and profound humiliation, I threw in the towel and moved across the country, accepting a faculty position at Simpson University in Redding, California.

My mistake wasn't in leaving. It was in believing that a geographical relocation would resolve the disintegration taking place in my emotional life. I was applying a Band-Aid where surgery was needed. In desperation I put my tail between my legs, packed up my family, and hauled my unhealed past three thousand miles across the country.

California Screamin'

Despite what had happened, I was convinced California would offer wonderful opportunities for ministry. Still hoping to make a difference for the Lord, I planned to teach at Simpson and also plant a church in the community. Perhaps a breakneck pace would keep my anxiety at bay.

Cheryl and I bought a small hobby ranch outside town. Though the kids thrived, our marriage almost didn't survive. I had taken Cheryl thousands of miles away from her family; planted her on a barren hilltop in a house without neighbors; surrounded her with dogs, ducks, goats, and a horse, while I began burning the candle at both ends trying to prove my significance.

Teaching at Simpson was a profound disappointment. It wasn't that my colleagues weren't great. They were the salt of the earth, dedicated to changing lives. The problem was mine. Leaving the seminary had been a devastating loss that I had neither fully admitted nor grieved. Nor was I able to acknowledge my regret at having accepted the leadership position in the first place. I had loved teaching and developing meaningful relationships with students. That had been my sweet spot, the place where I knew I was making a difference. I had compromised everything because of an opportunity to climb the ladder. Now I'd lost that position. Forever.

The graduate program at Simpson was just developing, so I went from having forty or fifty students in my classes to four or five. I was also assigned to teach required freshman courses to teenagers who were fresh out of high school and unhappy about being forced to take Bible classes. Instead of being the lead dog at a recognized theological seminary, I was the new guy on the second floor.

My office was the size of a broom closet, complete with a wooden desk propped up by a book under one leg. There was a folding chair and a board placed on two rusty brackets to hold my library.

The noise I made as I fell down the ladder of success created an emotional sonic boom, even if I was the only one who heard it. Had I been honest, I would have admitted that I was furious about what had happened. The loss I had suffered was like a compound fracture in my soul. If I'd been secure with the Lord, I would have told him exactly what I thought about the whole mess. But I was still afraid my mother might be right—that Jesus was standing by, ready to take my head off if I set a foot out of line.

Though I played nice on the outside, inside I was dancing with depression to the beat of a song whose lyrics were all about frozen rage.

Instead of dealing with the wounds that haunted me, I did my best to ignore them. My inability to acknowledge the source of my issues meant that I needed to develop a different narrative about what was happening. I figured God was turning his back on me until I could get my act together and prove I was worth hanging around. It was my plan to do that very thing. Before arriving in California I had received permission to plant a new church near Simpson. It didn't matter that there were already a couple of other churches from the denomination there. One more wouldn't hurt. At least that's what I thought.

One of my brightest students from Alliance had decided to bring his family west to help plant this new church. Together we would use our gifts to develop a cutting-edge ministry that would radically change lives. Having taught church planting, I felt confident we could do something good for the Lord.

The church we wanted to plant was to be contemporary in style and open to a more expressive form of spirituality. We were hungry to see people come to Christ, experience the ministry of the Holy Spirit, and develop disciples who believed Jesus was still in the business of changing lives and healing people. At the core of the church would be small groups where people felt safe and valued as unique children of God.

The two of us threw ourselves into the task with everything we had. Meeting with area denominational leaders, running down marketing contacts, looking over potential locations for the church, and talking to people interested in what we were doing consumed our time. Before long, we had gathered a small group of people, and then a crowd started to form. A few families moved across the country to be part of what we were doing. Every Wednesday night a growing group of people gathered at our house to worship, pray, and learn principles of the kingdom of God.

In a matter of weeks, we outgrew our house and began to meet in the back room of a warehouse. Before we knew it, our little tribe had become a small movement in the community, and within eighteen months we had a thriving church with more than eight hundred people attending services and becoming part of small groups. The church became the talk of the town and drew the attention of a few Christian leaders nationally. After the church was written up in a couple of magazines, people began visiting to discover what was happening. Several pastors in need of restoration moved to the community to become part of the church.

By any standard, our new church was a success, one of the most exciting things I had ever experienced in ministry. I was grateful for the young pastor who yoked with me and also for many others who caught the vision and dug in alongside us. In less than two years we went from being a handful of folks praying on my back porch to one of the largest churches in the denomination.

Beneath the wonder and magic of such a powerful movement of grace, I was barely keeping it together. Physical and emotional exhaustion were setting in quickly, and the disconnection between Cheryl and me only made things worse. I couldn't understand how it was possible to live in a place of such extremes. God was pouring out his grace abundantly even while I was falling apart inside.

Instead of *A Tale of Two Cities,* it was *A Tale of Two Terrys.* I was smack in the middle of my own "best of times, worst of times" narrative, and it felt awful. There were days when I thought I couldn't handle one more thing, good or bad. I had no idea how much worse things were about to get.

Not everyone in the denomination celebrated the rapid growth of the church. Some were suspicious of our more open stance toward the ministry of the Holy Spirit. A few of the local pastors started speaking against me; it was just like what had happened at Alliance.

Crazy rumors began to circulate about what we did during our services, and calls grew for me to be examined theologically by leaders within the denomination.

This fresh opposition revved up members of the old guard who had opposed me at the seminary in New York, and a second round of attacks soon gained steam. One day the president of Simpson pulled me into his office to tell me that he would have to fire me if the controversy continued.

Soon I was summoned to a meeting of leaders who would decide whether I fit the theological mold traditionally held by the denomination. They spent six hours grilling me. I tried humbly to show that everything I taught was in line with the Bible as well as with the organization's historic doctrines. Though I silenced the mob for a time and won a few friends in the process, the pressure took me one step closer to the edge.

Is That a Light at the End of the Tunnel or a Locomotive Barreling Toward Me?

Not long afterward I received a telephone call from the dean at Alliance Theological Seminary, who invited me to return to Nyack to teach a one-week summer intensive course. He also mentioned that he wanted me to consider rejoining the faculty. I was ecstatic. It seemed that God was responding to the cry of my heart, restoring what had been stolen.

Cheryl wasn't convinced, but she agreed to at least consider the idea.

When summer came I packed everyone into the car to head east. The plan was to go home to visit relatives and then drive to Nyack for a week of teaching. Cheryl and our two girls would stay behind with her parents while my teenage son, Aaron, joined me for a week in our old stomping grounds. While I taught, he would run with his old pals, an experience I hoped would convince him it was time to move back.

The class went great. With a room packed full of students, I was in my own skin again, and all systems were go. My colleagues were thrilled that I would consider returning to the seminary, and my nightly calls to Cheryl finally convinced her that this was the right move for our family. I was having the time of my life.

On the next to last night, the dean invited me to dinner, bringing along a couple of my old pals from the administration. We talked about old times, laughed, and connected at levels I hadn't experienced in quite some time. It seemed like the rebirth of joy. But the mood shifted as dinner came to a close.

"Terry, I have some bad news for you," he intoned. "The guys know, so this is no surprise to them."

I heard the sound of pounding. Was it from someone knocking the legs out from under me?

"I am not permitted to offer you a contract. You have become too controversial, and leadership believes it will hurt the institution. I'm sorry. This is not what I wanted."

As the blood rushed from my head, I felt faint, grabbing the edge of the table to steady myself. My body went numb as I fought to catch a breath. Tears formed in my eyes, and I stared at the dean in disbelief. This couldn't be happening to me, not again. But it was.

After a sleepless night, I taught the last day of class out of pure determination. At five o'clock I dismissed the students, said my goodbyes, turned off the lights, and took my first step into an unbearable dark night of the soul.

Staggering back to the apartment in despair, I hoped I could tumble into bed and sleep the pain away. Instead, I began having panic attacks. Explosion after explosion of fear surged through my body, rendering me helpless. I thought I would die of a heart attack but was too paralyzed to do a thing about it. I wanted to run but my legs wouldn't move.

I waited for Aaron to return. The wide-eyed look on his face told me that my condition frightened him. That night my sixteen-year-old son stayed in the bed holding me, afraid to go to sleep for fear I would do something to myself. By morning I was barely able to form a sentence. Aaron packed up our bags and loaded the car. I asked him to drive since I was tired. The truth was I couldn't get behind the wheel even had I wanted to.

After picking Cheryl and the girls up, we headed to California. On the trip back I was free falling, drowning in depression, and enraged that I had to return to Redding to a life I didn't want. Panic attacks began to chase me by the hour.

We arrived home, and I had to preach the next day. Somehow I did. People were affectionate and enthusiastic about whatever it was I said. After church, I went to bed, and Cheryl spent most of the afternoon lying beside me.

With the shades pulled down to block the light, I spent the next four weeks in the bedroom. Depression called out to its sick friend agoraphobia, and I was frozen in irrational fear. Though I was under a doctor's care, nothing seemed to help. For the entire summer I stayed home, too afraid even to walk to the end of the lane. The church gave me a leave of absence, and I cut myself off from everyone, lost in a darkness too deep to describe.

God was nowhere to be found. Life felt meaningless. Overwhelmed, Cheryl asked my parents to travel across the country to help her take care of things around the house. They were shocked when they saw me. Mom cried. Dad brought me a gift from a truck stop along the highway, a Louis L'Amour novel titled *The Trail to Crazy Man*.

Perfect.

Ten

LOCKED UP

The building loomed over us, less than sixty feet away. Constructed of gigantic sandstone blocks blackened as though they had survived a great fire, the structure was cold, gothic, and in need of repair.

I approached slowly with my head down and eyes leaking tears. Cheryl walked beside me. My chronic troubles had left her feeling emotionally disconnected. When I stopped in the middle of the sidewalk, reluctant to move forward, her face revealed a mixture of frustration and panic. There were less than twenty steps left. Easy steps along a concrete walkway, level ground leading into the main building. But I felt too frightened to advance and too sick to turn back. What lay behind had been painful, but what lay ahead scared me to my core. To enter the compound we had to walk through a guarded opening in the wrought-iron fence that surrounded the five-acre campus. Ten feet tall and spiked at the top, it formed an impenetrable barrier erected to keep people from escaping. I would soon be one of the lost souls locked behind its bars.

Despite drastic measures over the last several months, my emotional upheaval wouldn't let up. In fact, it only seemed to get worse in the midst of prayer and medical treatment. Though the psychiatric hospital had been my idea, I wondered what would happen once I passed through those doors. Would my theology, my relationship with God, and my sense of self survive the experience?

Friends and family had weighed in with unsolicited advice: "get more rest," "go back to work," "change your diet," "pray more," "memorize Scripture," "get deliverance from demons," "think positive," "increase your medicine." I tried everything but remained stuck, unable to emerge from the darkness and find my way to a place of light. My disappointment over not improving only added to the despair I felt. It seemed I couldn't even heal right.

Regardless of my efforts, the darkness didn't flinch when I opened the Bible and seemed to laugh at the suggestion that doubling down on prayer would set me free. Something inside me was so broken that traditional spiritual disciplines didn't touch it.

Against the wishes of my physician and my family, I decided to admit myself to Cedar Springs, a psychiatric hospital in Colorado Springs. Colleagues had warned me not to take this step, saying it would ruin my ministry if the news ever got out. But I was fighting for my sanity, not thinking about ministry.

Though the thought of being locked up in a mental hospital was humiliating, I didn't know what else to do. If someone had told me that smearing peanut butter on my forehead every morning would help, my only question would have been “chunky or creamy?”

I had heard about the hospital from a friend who had preceded me on a journey into the night. An organization named Rapha operated a Christian unit at the hospital that was renowned for treating hurting people. My friend said it had helped him, and help was all I was looking for because healing seemed out of reach. Recapturing a bit of sanity would have been worth the price of admission, astronomical though it was.

I finally stepped through the iron gateway and entered the building through the glass doors leading into the unit. Inside was a reception area with three small chairs and a nurse’s station behind a sliding window. To the left were two large wooden doors, magnetically locked, with the entry and exit controlled by whoever sat at the desk.

Cedar Springs was an inpatient lockdown facility for people at the end of their ropes. Once I passed through its doors, Cheryl and everyone else I knew and loved would be on the outside while I would live on the inside with people like me who could no longer keep the past at bay. The admitting nurse asked for a signature stating that I was voluntarily admitting myself and that I would abide by the rules of the institution. I wanted to cry but was afraid that if I started I would never stop. Taking the pen in hand, I scribbled an illegible signature.

After fighting so hard to escape my crazy-making childhood, living through a rebellious youth, beating the odds by attending college and seminary, becoming a successful pastor and then an up-and-coming Christian leader, was this how everything would end?

Weak-kneed and dragging my shattered heart with me, I passed through the wooden doors and then submitted to the required search. Everything I had, toiletries and personal items, was placed in a box, available only when I signed them out at the nurse's station. There would be no such thing as privacy because from that moment on a member of the staff would hover nearby, regardless of what I was doing. At night aides would shine a bright light into my bedroom at thirty-minute intervals to ensure I had not hurt myself.

Though Cedar Springs was intended as a place of healing, first impressions brought that into question. Shortly after signing myself in, I wanted out. But it was too late. I had already heard the doors clang shut behind me like the steel jaws of a giant bear trap.

I belonged to them now.

That night I sat on the edge of my bed and cried uncontrollably. I had traveled thirteen hundred miles to reach this hospital and wondered if it would be a far longer journey to find my way home. In a brief moment of sanity, I remembered words spoken by Nazi prison camp survivor Corrie ten Boom: "The object of your greatest pain can become the source of your greatest blessing when you offer it to God." I said my first prayer in a long time. *Lord, if you're even there, use this.*

For the next month I received counseling, participated in group therapy, and met with my psychiatrist. I ate, slept, and cried more often than I care to admit. The people who served me were wonderful, and the clinical director eventually became one of my dearest friends. But the experience was a long journey into emotional pain as I began digging into my past like an archaeologist looking for some remnant of a hidden narrative, waiting for the aha moment that would make sense out of my story.

Mornings began with a psychologist *talking* about the consequences of being performance driven, followed by individual counseling where I had to *talk* about my personal problems, which led to group sessions where everyone had a chance to *talk* about the difficulties they were facing. This concluded with a staffing review, in which the professionals would *talk* about how I was doing.

Even though I was beginning to understand how I had ended up in such a state, starting with my hardscrabble childhood followed by a life of hyperperformance, I was clueless about how to change. All the talk, no matter how revealing it was, didn't result in any obvious transformation.

The most healing aspect of the entire experience was the time spent with other patients. Locked in a psych hospital, up to our necks in emotional pain, we were ready to drop the pretense. During the evenings we often sat shoulder to shoulder on a couch holding on to one another for dear life. This was our healing spot, a place where we cried, listened, and laughed.

Will You Be My Valentine?

One evening after dinner I noticed a couple at the nurse's station. He was a mountain of a guy dressed like a man who spent most of his days on a tractor. The woman was in her mid- to late sixties, wearing a simple cotton dress and clutching a patent leather handbag from another time and place. The sun had not been kind to her complexion, and her gray hair was pulled back tightly into a bun that fought to stay perched on top of her head.

The man offered only mumbled replies to the questions pressed on him by the admissions nurse. Fiddling with the hat he held in his massive hands, he looked like he wanted to be anywhere but where he was. Shifting back and forth in his chair, he never made eye contact and kept glancing toward the main door whenever he could. His body language shouted that being here was not his idea.

The woman sat beside him, wiping her tears with an embroidered handkerchief, occasionally nodding whenever questions were directed her way. Nervously surveying the terrain, she looked over to where I was seated, turning away as soon as she thought I had noticed.

I felt sorry for both of them. It had been only two weeks since I had been in that same heart-crushing space. In just moments one of them would walk away, while the other would be left to wonder when and if he or she would step beyond those locked doors back into the known world.

The woman, who I will call Lois, was admitted to the hospital that evening. The next day we learned she was battling depression. Several days went by with her saying very little in group therapy. Most of the time she hung her head like a whipped dog. Tears were her most common response to questions that came her way.

Lois hid in her room after the evening meal and didn't join the rest of us on the lifeboat that folks from the outside would call a couch. We decided to give her space, thinking that time, patience, and a full measure of compassion might help her peek out from under her shell and join the rest of us "crazies" in our evening ritual. Before long, Lois squeezed in beside us for the nightly routine of listen, love, and laugh.

One evening, she took a risk, broke the silence, and began to share a story. Some on the outside might have thought it trite, given the issues that had brought each of us to that place. But no one there did. We listened carefully, glad that she was beginning to unpack the baggage weighing down her soul. Together, we honored the moment as sacred space.

At first she hesitated, embarrassed that her tale was not worth everyone's time. One of the women held her hand and encouraged her to continue, and Lois told the story. It was a February day long past and nearing Valentine's Day. Her fourth-grade teacher had given the students folders they were to color as part of the art lesson for the week.

On Valentine's Day, the students were to bring in handmade cards for all the other kids and place them on the teacher's desk. During recess, the cards would then be slid into the appropriate folders, with the children returning to find theirs filled with cards.

Given the poverty she knew at home, Lois was thrilled at the thought of receiving these construction paper gifts. After pacing the playground, she dashed into the classroom as soon as the bell sounded, making straight for her desk. Kids were scrambling through their folders to see what they received.

At this point in her story, Lois began to sob, not as a woman in her late sixties might cry, but as a little girl about to speak the unspeakable. As she lifted the brightly colored folder from her seat and looked inside, she saw not a single valentine. No student had placed one with her name on the teacher's desk that day. She stared into the gift of nothingness.

Tears formed around our circle as Lois fell into the lap of the woman holding her hand. Her story had touched a raw place in all of us. No one said "It will be okay" or "That was not a big deal," or, even worse, told a story of greater loss. We sat in shared sorrow not only for our friend Lois but also for ourselves. Together we shared the only thing we had—our loss, our touch, and the honor of hearing the story of what had broken her heart.

As I lay in bed that night, I could not get Lois out of my mind. The next morning I called Cheryl, who was staying with friends in Colorado Springs. Though it was October, I asked her to find a package of children's valentines and bring them the next day, along with a folder.

When the opportunity arose, I shared my plan with other members of the Fellowship of the Couch. One person decorated the folder, while the rest of us filled out valentines with our names and special notes to Lois. When evening came, as we returned to our sacred space, we presented the surprise gift to our hurting friend. The folder was a gift of love from people who were barely holding themselves together. As we fought to heal Lois, we moved closer to wholeness ourselves.

Lois cried like a baby, fingering every valentine as though each were a priceless gem. Her sobbing had a different quality now because hope was being reborn in her tears. Soon she would have the courage to tell other stories that would be honored just as this one had been. The valentines we gave her that night couldn't erase the loss she had suffered long ago, but they could create a new grid of expectation for Lois. All of us found a little more hope that night.

The next evening we laughed with Lois when she informed us that her counselor thought she was starting to respond to therapy because she was beginning to sound more hopeful. She hadn't mentioned what had happened the night before because, in her words, "It was too special to talk about."

It seemed clear to me that the change in Lois was produced not merely by talking to her therapist but also by having a new experience of generosity that had touched the wound inside her. What had made the vital difference was the experience of deep connection with others who cared about her and who had affirmed the importance of her feelings.

That experience with Lois planted a seed in my mind: *It takes more than concepts to set a heart free. It takes the power of a new experience, which then gives birth to a new story.*

Crazy Fun

After a couple of weeks, I was able to get a three-hour pass to leave campus along with two other patients. Before the nurse disengaged the magnetic doors, everyone shouted at us to bring back some movies. After enjoying dinner at a Chinese restaurant, we stopped at the local video store—remember those?

"We'd like to rent these movies," said one of my new friends, handing the videos to the woman behind the counter.

"Of course," she said. "Do you have a membership here?"

"No, sorry, I don't."

"No problem. Just give me your address, and we'll rent them to you."

With split-second brilliance, my friend turned the moment on its head. Fixing her with a thousand-yard stare, he slowly intoned, "Our address is Cedar Springs Psychiatric Hospital." Looking at me, he said, "He writes books and I fly jet planes."

The woman gave us an eye-popping stare and then explained that she had to talk to her manager. After she disappeared into the office, we doubled over laughing. Possibly the funniest part was that everything he had said was essentially true. Once "psychiatric hospital" was mentioned, she could only imagine the worst.

Later that night we sat on the couch with other patients, roaring over *What About Bob?,* a movie about a mental patient who was more normal that the psychiatrist who treated him. It seemed clear to us that the main difference between folks on the inside and those on the outside is just that. It's a matter of location. Everyone has their stuff.

Back in the Real World

After a month at the hospital, I returned to Redding. Though I didn't resume teaching at Simpson, the church elders agreed to a graduated increase in responsibilities. The road ahead was treacherous, and progress was of the two-steps-forward-one-step-back variety. Though the depression had begun to lift, my chronic anxiety was as strong as ever.

During my stay in the hospital, I had learned a great deal about psychological disorders. But mere knowledge wasn't enough to heal me. The staff at Rapha had emphasized the importance of memorizing truth and aligning my life accordingly. So day and night I carried a small notebook filled with scriptures. I treated it as if it were a golden tablet handed down by the archangel Michael himself.

When things got tough, I fingered through every page, hoping to land on the one truth that would push back the storm. That notebook became so worn and beat up that it looked like something a dog had dug up in the yard. Like a tin of Skoal, it had left its mark on my back pocket, but my soul went pretty much untouched.

By now I had learned something I was afraid to admit to anyone, especially myself. Though the Scriptures were true, they didn't hit me as real. Just reading them didn't bring me a life-changing, gut-level response. I knew it was a terrible thing to say about God's Word, but I also knew I had to be honest. Even though I loved the Bible, my investment in keeping Scripture close wasn't paying the dividends I had hoped.

The unhealed memories from my past were real events that were still alive inside me. Those unrepaired ruptures had a personal story attached to them, a story that engaged my senses, evoked unforgettable feelings, and left painful images of people and actions forever etched into my psyche.

Being beaten down the stairway by my mother was an experience permanently wired into the neuro-pathways of my brain. I was able to reengage every element of that nightmare, from sights, sounds, and sensations to the message it left on body and soul. That wound had left a mark, giving rise to the idea that I was someone who only created more work for her. That idea nagged at my soul, evoking feelings of worthlessness and fear.

I had tried various strategies to deal with the wounds of my childhood traumas, but nothing seemed to work. Though I'd abandoned overtly sinful strategies for dealing with the pain, the problems persisted no matter how much truth I threw at them.

On a conceptual level, I believed Scripture was true. But simply repeating that truth wasn't enough. I needed a real encounter that would change what I believed about myself, one that would heal memories of the past that were still kicking and screaming inside me.

Though I knew the idea would freak out some in the Christian community, I flat out needed an experience with Jesus. I longed for an episode with him that would reach into my wounded history and clean out the leftover debris.

I wanted the Holy Spirit to go back into my broken past like a disaster-relief team and deal with the mess my childhood trauma had left behind.

Eleven

DISASTER RELIEF

Several months after returning from the hospital, I was holed up in the Sierra Nevada mountains at a friend's cabin, enjoying the warmth of the fire I had just built in the Franklin stove. Snow was falling on a dense thicket of tall pines standing sentinel outside as the temperature dropped below freezing. Wrapped up in quilts, Cheryl and I snuggled into large overstuffed chairs. I was living through the cold fog of chronic anxiety, though brief moments of clarity were sparking fresh hope.

Though I was having a hard time hanging on to the Lord, I began to suspect that he was holding on to me. That was enough to help me think that one day I might be restored. I had been doing my best to get better, redefining my role at the church, developing a new rhythm of rest and work, seeing a counselor weekly, and attacking my diet with a vengeance. Refusing to leave a single stone unturned,

I even gave up chocolate and caffeine, proof that I was serious about my recovery!

But if it was a race toward wellness, an inchworm would have outdistanced me. Though I tried to align my thinking with God's Word, I was disappointed in how little my efforts impacted my feelings. I could rattle off scriptures as fast as a livestock auctioneer and could articulate theological truths as intelligently as the scarecrow from the *Wizard of Oz,* but little of this influenced the underworld of my wounded soul.

Though I believed in my head that God's words were true, the unprocessed wounds of my past seemed more real. Instead of lining up behind the promises of Scripture, my feelings lined up behind the pain I felt. "Real" held more power over my emotions than did "true." That only brought more guilt and shame.

I understood that my battle came from the trauma I had suffered early in my life. Witnessing death and being repeatedly shamed can do that to a kid, birthing a toxic way of seeing things. Though that was a fact, no amount of words would help. I needed something else.

Merely understanding where my problems had originated wasn't enough to heal me. My inability to process the hurts inflicted by my dysfunctional past had locked me into a prison of anxiety. But I didn't have the key to get out of jail.

Looking out at the whirling snow, I longed for help but felt worn ragged from asking. The Bible I held in my hand seemed like more of a talisman than God's living Word. Even so, a voice deeper than my own nudged me to crack it open one more time. In unfeeling obedience, I did so. Instead of slogging through Paul's letters or reengaging the teachings of Jesus, I chose something closer to where I was living—the story of Jesus and Gethsemane. That seemed to fit.

For the first time in a long time, I had a visceral reaction to what I was reading. Though I'd read the story dozens of times before, something particular stuck out to me. The night before his death, Jesus had poured out his anguish to his Father in complete honesty. Even his body reflected the agony he felt. Sweating drops of blood, Jesus was overwhelmed with sorrow to the point of death.

This time through the story, I was struck by the way the Father responded. Instead of handing Jesus a spiral notebook filled with Bible verses and saying, "Here, Son, memorize this text," God took a different approach. He knew something far more powerful was needed to address the agony of Gethsemane. So he gave his beloved Son an *experience* that assured him of his love, dispatching angels to strengthen him.

In the midst of Jesus's overwhelming need, the promises of God had to become real for him, for only the Real could strengthen and sustain him. Gethsemane was his great dark night of the soul.

I had always been told that a Christian should never seek an experience but should only trust in God's Word. Viewing the story with fresh eyes made me long to experience God's Presence in the midst of my own deep struggles. I realized that Jesus had been given an experience of grace while he was seeking his Father's help.

This was what I longed for in my own life. Though my struggles were nothing compared to the cosmic struggles Christ endured in Gethsemane, my chronic anxiety was the cross bearing down on my own weary back. Since it was experiences of trauma that had cut my heart out, I couldn't stop hoping that another kind of experience might make me whole again.

As I read and reread the narrative in that snug mountain cabin, I began to unpack its treasures. I realized that Jesus had gone away to a special place to cry out for his Father's touch. He didn't open up on the streets of Jerusalem, at a dinner with friends, or in the midst of a busy season of ministry. He chose to go to that mountain garden in order to seek his Father. Gethsemane was both a sacred space and a place of safety for Jesus. So that became my starting point, finding a sacred and safe place in which to seek God's touch.

Instead of taking a crowd along with him, Jesus invited only a few trusted friends to Gethsemane. Once there, he asked only Peter, James, and John to continue on to that place of agony and heartache. Even though his disciples had blown their assignment, I got the point.

I wondered who I should ask to journey with me into the dark place of my unprocessed wounds. Out of the crowd in my life, who could I trust to walk with me through the storm? It had to be those who honored vulnerability, extended generous grace, and understood that confidentiality is an essential ingredient of healing.

I realized, too, that when Jesus poured out his heart to the Father, he did it with complete honesty. His uncensored honesty gave me permission to unpack the desperation locked up inside me.

Reading and praying over that passage yielded other insights. Somewhere in that Gethsemane night, the Father spoke to Jesus, enabling him to rise strong enough to move ahead to Calvary. Though the Bible doesn't disclose the details of what transpired, it seems clear that it wasn't an intellectual exercise that lifted Jesus to his feet. Gethsemane was a profound spiritual experience, full of sensation, feeling, interaction, grief, honesty, and divine intervention. The Father had enveloped the Son with his Presence, and Christ was able to surrender into that embrace. I longed to surrender to it as well.

Reading the Bible that night in a cabin nestled deep in the Sierra Nevadas seemed to make my own pathway to healing clear. The Holy Spirit seemed to be inviting me to journey into my past to find freedom for my future. It was time for me to begin experiencing the disaster relief I had longed for. The Gethsemane prayer would be my guide through the darkness.

When the Past Is Present

After my time in the mountains, I began reading books on memory, behavioral science, neurobiology, and inner-healing prayer. I was profoundly impacted by the short phrase *mental time traveler* from Endel Tulving, an experimental psychologist and neuroscientist. Tulving showed that it is possible for people to reexperience memories as a way to process the unhealed past.

If that were true, it occurred to me that I could reexperience my unprocessed wounds and un-grieved losses, not just as painful flashbacks, but as experiences in which I could encounter God's healing touch, as Jesus did in Gethsemane.

Scripture tells us that God is not bound by time because he exists in eternity. Because of his transcendence, he can touch the wounds of our past with a real experience of his Presence. Our part is to open ourselves to his healing touch and walk back in time to process those wounds with him.

By following the story of Jesus in the Garden of Gethsemane, I started to construct a framework for deep healing. I knew I needed two things to begin. First, a safe environment in which to meet the Lord, and second, safe people who could love and care for me on the journey. The importance of safety was reinforced by something I'd learned in Psych 101 during my freshman year of college. Jean Piaget, the renowned Swiss psychologist, pointed out that the first step in therapy begins with helping the broken feel safe. Piaget believed that processing emotional pain should never proceed until safety is first established. Since I hadn't felt safe either on the inside or the outside for many years, I was all in for such an approach.

Once safety was established, I could then ask the Holy Spirit to unearth an unprocessed story from the distant past. It seemed important to let God guide me, trusting him to show me which memories he wanted to deal with and when. He wasn't asking me to take a pick and shovel and dig through my past. Instead he was inviting me to allow him to bring to the surface of my mind the memory most in the way of my healing journey.

I knew unprocessed memories were often accompanied by strong emotions. My part would be to allow myself to fully experience and express whatever emotions surfaced, not trying to censor or control them. That way I could grieve the loss instead of ignoring or minimizing it.

Allowing feelings to resurface would be helpful in another way as well. Though many people fear being misled by their emotions, I began to realize that feelings never lie. They are always true in the sense that they accurately reflect whatever it is I am thinking. Of course, what I'm thinking might be based on a lie, but my feelings could help to unmask the lie.

So there would be no stuffing, no censoring, no ignoring, as I allowed myself to reexperience painful events of the past.

I believed that God wanted to lead me in a time of prolonged healing. I decided to put my plan into action with the Spirit's help.

My Healing Journey

After developing the framework for healing, I laid it out with a couple of trusted colleagues who had experience with healing and asked if they would be willing to prayerfully walk with me into the past.

One of the first memories the Holy Spirit brought to mind was the "horse---t for brains" incident. I had thought that multiple academic degrees had vanquished that particular lie, but I was wrong. It had left its mark on my sense of self. I often fought feelings of inferiority and shame, which affected my assessment of my ability to articulate the gospel.

One day my friends joined me in the safety of my study. As we prayed together, and with the help of the Holy Spirit, I allowed myself to travel back in time to the living room of my childhood home where Mom had pronounced those hurtful words. It may have been in my imagination, but I was there just the same, registering every detail. I was not remembering feelings but reexperiencing them.

I was amazed at how quickly the experience with my mother

went from the hilarity of listening to Carrot's tall tales to the shock of public humiliation. I felt the emotions still present within me. Shame rose up, threatening to expose me as a fraud. Then tremendous anger surfaced as I relived the mocking laughter that followed her rebuke.

As my friends and I prayed, I reexperienced the rage I felt as she read out my grades from my report card, still feeling as though I wanted to burn the house down in retaliation. Emotion boiled out in waves of outrage mixed with crushing sadness.

Not once did the Lord ask me to put a pretty face on what was happening. I expressed my feelings in the uncensored way they had formed a long time ago, foul words and all. Then, in a powerful moment of transformation, I was able to "see" the Lord enter the living room with me. I was stunned.

In the sanctity of my imagination, Jesus came to my side and enfolded me in his loving arms. Tenderly, he said, *Terry, I am saddened this happened to you. They're wrong.* Waves of disappointment and pain poured from my wounded soul as I collapsed against his chest.

Jesus placed his hand gently upon my forehead and a rush of Presence came over me, cleansing me of the offense I had carried for so many years. With his touch I knew there was nothing wrong with my mind. Words of Scripture flashed into my thoughts and became suddenly real. *You have the mind of Christ* was what I heard Jesus say. That day, Jesus walked the teenage me out of that wounded memory, and I never had to struggle with it again.

My healing encounter had involved more than a Bible verse conceptually delivered. It was an experience of Presence that forever changed the way I saw that terrible day. Once again my worst day had become my best day, a miracle of transformation that happened when Jesus stepped into my story and healed a toxic memory.

After that, a long journey commenced, one that began to free me from the prison of my unhealed past. As memories of trauma surfaced, even when I was alone, I was able to meet the Lord and experience a deep, step-by-step release, one that concept-driven behavioral science didn't touch. After what had seemed like a never-ending season of mourning, joy began to break into my heart like dawn's first light.

Regardless of the fact that I was getting better, I knew that some would question what had happened, rejecting the use of imagination as a tool for emotional healing. But the Bible is full of picture language, images of mustard seeds growing, fish gathered into nets, sheep carried on a loving shepherd's shoulders, and a mother hen gathering her fearful brood under her wings, all for the purpose of engaging truth episodically. So why not extend that to meeting Christ in the unprocessed past? Since Jesus could step across time, he surely could walk into my imagination and heal my past. What's more, the message I had heard from him about having his mind was completely consistent with Scripture.

How often I had allowed my mind to run away with dark images of rejection and judgment, each time resulting in emotional despair. They played out in my mind like my own personal *film noir.* I was a living example of Paul's warning that the mind controlled by the flesh was death.

Now I learned to turn to the Holy Spirit and ask him to use my imagination to picture the healing touch of Christ in my unprocessed past. Those pictures, grounded in the truth of Scripture, became instruments of the Holy Spirit's transforming presence in my life.

Following this process began to set me free, drawing me into deeper intimacy with the Lord and birthing an even greater love for his Word and his kingdom. Many of the wounding experiences that surfaced had generated false beliefs about me, with more than a few also about God and others. In the process, I discovered two destructive beliefs deeply embedded in my wounds. The first was that I would never measure up. The second was that God was out to get me. If I wanted to be free, I needed to face those false beliefs head on and with blunt honesty.

Buried feelings had driven me to adopt destructive behaviors in order to kill the pain, but in the end these only created more pain. Drugs and immorality were early weapons of choice. Later, I adopted performance and people-pleasing behaviors, ones that are often applauded. But these painkillers had only added more brokenness to my life.

My healing didn't happen overnight, but the days led to weeks, then months, and ultimately to years of deep emotional healing. Along the way, God opened doors for me to share my journey with other broken people. I was amazed at how it resonated. Whenever I presented the basic framework for deep emotional healing, people wanted more. Even though I freely admitted my time in a psychiatric hospital, people couldn't get enough.

Rather than repelling people, my breakdown seemed to attract them, adding credibility to what I was saying. I never dreamed that starting a talk with *I lost it and have the papers to prove it* would enable me to talk about the healing power of Christ. I began to think Corrie ten Boom had been right. God was turning the object of my greatest pain into the source of my greatest blessing. He was using my mess to bring healing to others.

A New Day Begins

Cheryl and I decided to invest in our future by moving from California to Colorado, where we received counseling and spiritual direction. We wanted our marriage to be pulled as tight as a zipper on a warm winter coat. Thinking my years as a pastor, seminary educator, church planter, and author were over, I got a temporary job in Colorado Springs as a handyman, replacing toilets in old houses.

One day I stopped in the office of a large Christian ministry in the city. I was standing out front waiting to pick up some material when a man came through the door and pointed at me. Other folks saw him barreling my way with his arm extended and finger waving wildly.

"Hey, I know you. You . . . you used to be somebody, didn't you?"

That wasn't the first time I'd heard a remark like that since falling down the ladder of success. A few months earlier it would have knocked me to my emotional knees. Now it was only an awkward moment. I took a deep breath and smiled.

Some time later I reconnected with my friend Pete Kuiper from Cedar Springs Hospital and told him about what I'd been experiencing. By now Pete was working at a hospital in Pueblo, Colorado, about forty miles from Colorado Springs. When he heard about the framework for deep healing, he asked me to share what I was learning with his staff.

Later he connected me with the famed baseball player Dave Dravecky and his wife, Jan, and I had the chance to walk their staff through the basic structure of healing. I spoke to them about the relationship between wounds, false beliefs, emotional upheaval, and the destructive choices people make in order to kill the pain of unhealed wounds.

By now life seemed a bit comical. By day I was fixing toilets and repairing holes in drywall, and by night I was speaking to caregivers and pastors about deep emotional healing. Maybe the two things had more in common than I thought! It wasn't a bad gig, especially since I had thought my ministry ended the day I walked into the psych hospital.

Looking back, I realize that my ministry indeed ended that day. The drive to be a superpastor, a well-known leader, and a church-growth star—all these false choices were abandoned behind two locked wooden doors. I had become like the men and women in the Bible who are known more for their brokenness than for their success.

As the Lord continued to pour grace straight through my wounded past, he began touching other lives. Instead of being doctor this and reverend that, I became "Terry, the agoraphobic depressive." That was okay by me because it spoke eloquently of the way Jesus was setting me free.

Twelve

UNCOVERING THE DEEPEST WOUND

It was four in the morning when I woke up. I had been bawling like a baby in my sleep, the tears staining my pillowcase and my nose running like tree sap in early spring. Disentangling myself from a knot of covers, I got out of bed and shuffled my way through the darkness to the bathroom of our rented townhouse in Colorado Springs.

Leaning on the edge of the sink with both arms, I shook my bowed head. Then I filled the basin with water and rested my hands in its warmth for a few moments in hopes of regaining my composure. Cupping my hands, I splashed water on my face, feeling it spill down my arms like rain falling from a leaky gutter. I looked in the mirror. An emotionally exhausted man stared back at me.

I was used to the bad dreams, but this one felt particularly painful. It had begun happily enough, with a surprise visit from my two eldest children. When Cheryl and I moved to Colorado with our youngest daughter, Emily, Cara and Aaron stayed behind in California to attend Simpson University. This was the first time we were living at such distance. My kids had always filled a deep place of loneliness I'd known since childhood. But now here they were in my dream, standing on our front porch smiling at me.

As I walked toward the townhouse, they ran to my side, hugged me, and told me they had come for a three-week visit. I was ecstatic. My heart flooded with peace as Cara held me, and I pressed my face to hers, enjoying the fragrance of her hair. Aaron kissed me on the cheek as he always did, and I could feel his unshaven face against mine. Like snow covering the ground on a soft winter's night, contentment settled over my soul. My three treasures—Cara, Aaron, and Emily—were here with me once again. For the next three weeks all would be well with the world.

Yet in the dream as quickly as the promise was made, it disappeared. Aaron and Cara said they had changed their minds and would be returning to California immediately. Instead of joy, I was left with a feeling of staggering loneliness that propelled me toward panic.

As the dream turned to bitter nightmare, I began to beg them, pulling them back into my embrace. But they fought against my grasp with the same intensity that drove me to pull them closer. Had they bent to my will, I would have never let them go. My pleas were shameless, and I began to cry.

My tears weren't those of a healthy father saying goodbye to his adult children. They were the cry of someone whose own heart had been buried beneath a pile of ungrieved losses. This was deep wailing from a boy who had never felt attached to anyone and who couldn't find a place to rest in safety.

As Aaron and Cara faded away into a mist of darkness, I cried out into the dense fog of my own hopelessness, *I will never feel whole without you.*

With that cry I startled awake, my heart pounding out of my chest, as desolate as if I had learned that someone I loved had died. Something unbalanced had been revealed in the night, the plea as bold in my mind as the words of Jesus in a red-letter Bible. Someone was speaking through the dream, but was it me, the Lord, or the Evil One? Or could it have been all three?

I knew about the dynamics of codependency, where the unfixed need a fixer and the unprotected a protector, where the runner begs for someone to chase him and the weak reach out for the strong. It's an unholy connection people make when they believe life will work only if someone else is willing to carry their emotional freight. Was that what this dream was about, my attempt to make my kids responsible for my well-being? While I realized the possibility, I recognized that something more was at work.

It seemed that layers of my internal world had begun peeling off one by one, revealing the core where the fire of my insecurity burned white hot. My dream haunted me for days as I tried to make sense of it.

Though my children helped to fill that deep place of loneliness I had carried inside since childhood, the last thing I wanted was for them to bear the burden of my emotional mess. If that was my subconscious expectation, I knew it had to stop immediately. Though it was natural to want them in my life, *needing* them for my well-being was dysfunctional and would hurt us all.

If someone had forced me to articulate what I was experiencing, I would have said, "I feel like I am unsafe on the inside and on the outside. The threat of separation from people I love ignites uncontrollable panic, which I do my best to hold in. But when it gets tapped, I can't seem to control it. Nothing can satisfy my longing to be secure."

I wanted to *not need* someone in order to be secure. It sounds like double-talk, but I knew there was truth in that jangle of words. I also knew that my dream hadn't been the first sign that the thought of separation terrified me, nor would it be the last.

Holding On for Dear Life

Memories began to surface. An especially painful one centered on a photo of me as a terrified child sitting in a stranger's lap. Though a single picture can be worth a thousand words, this one had elicited a thousand laughs from others and ten thousand screams from me. When I was a teenager, I hid it in a place where no one else would ever find it. To this day only the most trustworthy have ever glimpsed my photogenic shame.

It was nearing Christmas, soon after my fifth birthday. My mother had taken me to Gimbels department store in downtown

Pittsburgh to have my picture taken with Santa Claus. Because of my anxiety and my unfamiliarity with big city life, loud traffic and bustling crowds acted like accelerants, fueling my fear. Mom had to drag me out of the car, push me across the parking garage, pull me along the sidewalk, shove me through revolving doors, threaten me up the death-defying escalator, and force me into the line that led to the fat man. It didn't help that two of my mother's cousins were with us and that their kids seemed as excited as elves to see Santa.

Ignoring the black skid marks my shoes made as my feet dragged across the floor, Mom deployed her skills at shaming and comparing to move me past Santa's workshop and closer to the big man himself. Though I stiffened every muscle in my body, my mother managed to hike me onto Santa's lap for the coveted picture.

There I sat, clad in dark brown pants, white socks, black shoes, and a flannel cowboy shirt buttoned to the neck. I was scared out of my mind. The photographer set the shutter, inserted a new flash bulb, and told me to smile. A nanosecond before he pushed the button, I grabbed hold of my private parts with my left hand and held on for dear life. The picture that would haunt me for years to come was now a matter of permanent historical record.

I would love to say that Mom and Dad discarded that photo in order to protect their little boy from ridicule, but that would be a lie. Instead, they hauled it out every Christmas as though it were a cherished holiday memory to be shared with whoever happened to be present. Joining my parents in great howls of laughter were a host of relatives, including Grandma Mose and Uncle Fat. Neighbors were in on the joke too.

Not once did anyone seem to consider how this voyeuristic peep show might impact me. I hated that picture, the fat guy, my mother, every single person who laughed at me, and most certainly, that left hand.

Years later, when I looked at the photo, I felt my heart breaking for the little guy. It wasn't only about the stupid picture, but also about the terrible fear—the sheer terror of feeling unsafe and alone. The boy was clutching himself in a desperate effort at self-soothing because no one had heard his cry or cared about his pain. As I looked into his face, I knew exactly what he had believed. Nobody was there to protect him. There was no secure base to run to when the world seemed too big and scary. He was all alone.

One Thought and Panic Took Flight

A more recent memory surfaced. Cheryl and I had been sitting on the tarmac at Pittsburgh International, about to travel to Tulsa where I was to be the guest speaker at a megachurch in the city. It was our first time traveling by air without our children, who were still quite young. As the jet turned onto the runway, picking up speed for take-off, a thought flashed through my mind. *What if the airplane crashes and the kids need to be raised by my parents?* As the plane began to rise, I had a panic attack that almost blew my head off. It was everything I could do to remain in my seat.

The entire trip to and from Tulsa was horrible. I didn't say anything to Cheryl, partly due to embarrassment, and also because I didn't want to admit to myself how afraid I was. Since the panic attack occurred at takeoff, I associated the fear with flying, not with the thought about the kids. I would have preferred to walk home from Oklahoma rather than face the return flight.

It took years for me to realize that terror was ignited whenever that deep place of abandonment was touched. The trip to Oklahoma had been a double whammy because it involved the possibility of being separated from my children as well as the thought that my parents might have to raise them. Either idea was enough to send me into orbit. Together they launched a whole new level of fear.

Hot Dog Day

One of my least favorite memories was of a day we called Hot Dog Day. Every Thursday at noon, children from my elementary school lined up in the hallway. Grade by grade we marched single file into the church next door and down to the basement, where a platoon of ladies served two hot dogs, a small bag of chips, and a paper cup of soda to any child with a dollar bill. It was as traditional as the Fourth of July, only better because it happened every week.

One Thursday when I was a first grader, I took my place in line for Hot Dog Day with a single dollar bill crumpled in my sweaty little fist. As I hit the last step of the basement stairs, I looked over to the tables and saw my mother folding napkins. She had never been to Hot Dog Day before, so it took me by surprise. For some reason, the sight of her touched a deep place of loneliness, and I began to sob.

Instead of grabbing my hot dogs and chips along with the other students, I ran over to Mom and sat on her lap crying. Of course, I became the immediate center of attention and an object of ridicule. Laughter and "mommy's boy" chants erupted from my classmates, making matters worse. I hated myself for crying, but I couldn't stop the tears. The anxiety of separation came out uncontrollably.

Mom wasn't happy about the whole thing either. That night she made it clear that she would never go to Hot Dog Day again. Then she recounted every detail of what had happened, telling everyone how embarrassed she had felt when I had crawled onto her lap and bawled like a baby. Like all such stories in my life, she brought up Hot Dog Day whenever it served her purpose.

Years later, when Mom was traveling down some uncomfortable memory lanes, I asked why she had never come back for another Hot Dog Day. Her answer was telling. She said she just couldn't handle how my crying had stirred her up. Her nerves couldn't take that kind of emotion. She made the decision to avoid Hot Dog Days from then on because she didn't want to get "worked up" like that ever again.

Instead of attempting to help me deal with my own anxiety as many parents would have done, Mom was intent only on avoiding any upheaval in her own feelings. The way I felt wasn't even a blip on her radar.

No wonder the roles in our house were always flipped. Mom's unaddressed wounds kept my sister and me walking on eggshells. Instead of my mother attuning herself to us so that she could help modulate what was happening in our emotions, we had to do that for her. That meant Bonny and I were always on the alert, forced to read Mom's moods in order to anticipate her needs or to avoid making things worse. We tried hard to calm her when she got dialed up, to affirm her when she felt insecure, and to comfort her whenever an ungrieved loss proved too much for her to bear.

Abuse and neglect had left my mother without empathy even though she demanded sympathy from others. I knew the story of her difficult childhood by heart because she repeatedly talked about it. Whenever she brought it up, Bonny and I knew it was time to show her how bad we felt about what she had gone through. That left me wrestling with my inner chaos alone.

What I Should Have Gotten from Mom

As a young child, my longing to attach to Mom was a mixed bag. I never knew if drawing close would generate hugging or hitting. Though her responses were unpredictable, my desperation for connection always induced me to take the risk.

The emotional back and forth birthed all kinds of garbage in me, not the least of which was anxiety. It was a nightmare knowing that the person you wanted to run toward was also someone you needed to run from. I had no idea how to navigate that double bind. Later, I simply separated emotionally from Mom. But the longing for attachment didn't disappear. Instead, it played out in relationships, especially when I started dating, as I tried to get from others what I never got from Mom.

It took years for me to understand that my mother didn't have the reserves to be attentive to my emotional needs. Therefore, she couldn't use her strength to help my weakness or her stability to counter my insecurity. Without healthy bonding, my kid brain did not mature in ways that would have helped me get through tough times. That meant I didn't have the mental hardware on board to combat and process the effects of repeated trauma.

I was like a bird in perpetual flight, never able to find a nest in which to rest. To still the storm of separation anxiety, I fluttered from one relationship to the next, placing the burden of attachment where it could never be met. Instead of allowing God to develop a safe haven within my own soul, I tried to make the heart of another person that permanent place of security. The absence of a healthy childhood connection with either parent had created a grid for unhealthy dependencies upon others for my own well-being.

My Wake-Up Call

Like an early morning wake-up call, the message started coming through loud and clear. Childhood attachment issues were at the heart of my insecurity. There would be no deep healing unless these were touched and transformed. The journey began with my being willing to risk letting go of the heavy expectations I had unwittingly placed on those who loved me. Though the process was challenging, I soon found that the Lord was already working to fill a place in my soul that had been left untouched for years.

As only God could orchestrate, I stumbled into a friendship with Dr. Anne Halley, an expert on child development and attachment. She brought clarity to my understanding of attachment wounding. She also brought good news about the brain. Because of something called brain plasticity—the ability of the brain to change over time—my brain could be rewired. I began to realize that it's never too late to grow your brain.

Dr. Halley also helped me understand the relationship between disconnection from my mother and my inability to process chronic anxiety. Finally, I had some answers to the question, Why am I like this?

From her, I learned about the six core longings of every human heart. Like everyone else on the planet, I longed for

- love,
- security,
- understanding,
- purpose,
- significance, and
- belonging.

Without these core longings being met, I had fallen into a black hole of insecurity. Because of how wounded my mother's own heart had been, I couldn't survive without detaching from her. But that detachment disconnected me from hope.

In order to heal, I needed to experience God attaching me to himself in such a way that he could meet those needs. Through counseling and prayer I began to ask him to help me detach from unhealthy expectations so that I could attach to him in the deepest way possible. Getting there would be far from easy.

Thirteen

BACK TO REDDING

"You have got to be kidding me. Tell me this is a joke!"

My son, Aaron, had just dropped a bomb in the middle of the living room floor. The good news he had planned to deliver about his future plans landed like an incendiary device.

For the last several years, he and his wife, Destry, along with their two daughters, had been living near us in Ashland, Ohio, where Cheryl and I had relocated following a year of restoration in Colorado. When the door opened for me to join the faculty at Ashland Theological Seminary, it had seemed a perfect fit. On a slow road to recovery, we would enjoy a rhythm of life that supported healing.

Within a year of our arrival, Aaron and his wife decided to join us so that he could attend seminary. The next year our daughter Cara did the same. Our youngest daughter, Emily, was busy attending high school while living at home. It seemed a perfect setup for everyone.

Good things happened to our children in Ashland. They received great educations, landed important jobs, and found supportive friends. It's where Cara met and married her husband. It was also where Cheryl and I bought a farm and hosted Friday night sleepovers with our grandchildren. Though I still wrestled with anxiety, I was miles away from feeling trapped by it.

Now Aaron was putting everything at risk, threatening the good life we all enjoyed. My body language left little question regarding how I felt about the message he was trying to deliver. I coiled to strike and rattled a fair warning.

"Dad, I'm trying to tell you that I have taken a new job and we're moving. Don't make this any harder than it is."

My face registered anger as Aaron leaned back in his chair and took a deep breath. He had just delivered a gut punch, and I hadn't even seen it coming. Now my reptilian brain took over.

I leaned forward like a prosecuting attorney.

"Why? You have it made here. You're the assistant dean of religious life at the university. People stand in line for that kind of opportunity. You're throwing it all away?"

A more honest response would have been, *You're messing up my perfect world, and I don't appreciate it one bit. Don't you care that I'm holding on by my fingernails most days? How dare you take those babies of yours away from me!*

"Dad, I know this is hard," Aaron continued. "It's hard for me too. But Destry and I have prayed about it. This is the Lord, Dad; I know it."

Associating his decision with the Lord did nothing to defuse my ire. I pressed forward with the interrogation.

"So where is this job?"

He flinched as he blurted out the words.

"Dad, we're moving back to California."

As I fought to process this new information, the blood rushed to my head, my throat went dry, and I began to sweat. If my face wasn't beet red by then, I wasn't Terry Wardle. It was the closest thing to a panic attack I had experienced in several years, and I came out swinging.

"You'd do this to me? California? Why not tell me you're moving to the gates of hell? This can't be happening. You're willing to dig up that old wound?"

No Gold in California

Let me fill in some backstory.

One of the happiest days of my life had been the day I saw California in the rearview mirror. It wasn't as though everything had been bad there. Having a front-row seat when the church was exploding with growth and hundreds of people were coming to the Lord was a huge privilege. Cara and Aaron had thrived there. Loving people had supported me through my long nightmare. How could I not be grateful?

But California had also been the place where I had suffered an exhausting amount of opposition, a terrible breakdown, and a grueling recovery. No wonder I was thrilled the moment we crossed the Nevada line and headed toward Colorado.

Though California was yesterday's news, it had suddenly popped into the headlines again.

By now Aaron and I had transferred our sparring match to the barn. We were sitting in chairs facing each other. "Dad, this isn't about you. I mean, I know it hurts and all, but this is my life. I need this change, Dad. It's the right thing."

Then the news got worse.

"So where exactly in California?"

"Dad, we're moving back home to Redding. I've been offered the job as worship pastor at the church you started. I've already said yes and told the university I'm leaving."

Benedict Arnold could not have delivered more cutting news. This was betrayal pure and simple. Aaron was going back to the place I hated most, to the church where I had fallen apart, to stand shoulder to shoulder with some of the folks who had made life tough for me. In a selfish moment I looked at him and said, "I can't believe you'd do this to me, Aaron."

Flying out of his seat as if he'd been shot from a rocket, Aaron threw his chair across the floor and stomped out of the barn in tears.

I felt stunned. Though the barn was empty, I shouted, "I refuse to face another load of emotional crap!"

Not only had Ashland been good for my family, it was where my life and ministry had been restored. I had great friends and a spiritual director who was leading me deeper along the path of wholeness. I was also writing and speaking again. It was at Ashland that I had developed a ministry of formational prayer, a form of inner healing and spiritual formation aimed at broken men and women—and who is not broken?

I was on the most level footing I had been on for years. The last thing I needed was this mess.

Over the next several days, Aaron and I continued to talk, but nothing dissuaded him and nothing disarmed me. Even though I disagreed with his choice, I conceded that it was his decision to make. But he would have to walk out the consequences by himself.

"I will not be traveling to California to see you," I promised him. "I'll pay for you guys to come visit, but I will not be going there. So settle that in your mind right now."

The Trip to California

Even at a distance of two thousand miles, Aaron and I were able to mend the rift between us. But I held fast to my ultimatum. I had not returned to California, nor would I. That ironclad plan had to stay in place because it was the only thing keeping the water in my soul behind the dam. Of that I was certain.

My resolve lasted for eighteen months. Cheryl was the one who undermined it. Though she cared about how I felt, nothing was going to separate her from her children and grandchildren. By the next fall, despite my hissy fits, we were westward bound.

To survive the trip I began to develop a plan to manage the anxiety I felt about returning. I decided on three strategies. First, I would string together speaking engagements across the country, adopting a maybe-if-you-stay-busy-you-won't-notice-the-pain strategy. Second, I bought a convertible to enhance the cross-country drive. Third, Cheryl and I would take the entire family on vacation to Tahoe after spending only a few days in Redding.

For the months preceding the trip, my painkilling prescription worked pretty well. But as the date drew closer, I began to feel as though I were living on the ragged edge of a razor-sharp cliff. My expensive tranquilizers—speaking engagements, a sports car, and a vacation to Tahoe—had lost their mojo. Now it seemed I was facing round two in a bout of emotional breakdown. I could already feel the knockout punch to my gut.

The Lord knew about my anger not only because he already knows everything but also because I kept telling him about it. One morning, in the midst of my daily tirade, I heard him speak. The words were delivered with love, but they were firm. *Terry, you have left part of yourself behind in California. It is time. We are going back to bring him home.*

At these words, I wept uncontrollably. I had been fighting so hard, screaming, *Foul, unfair, don't you understand, this isn't right* and every other accusation that spilled over from the storm tearing me apart. But in that moment things began to slowly shift. Maybe the trip would not compromise my well-being. Perhaps it would be a journey of reclamation that would make me whole again.

It occurred to me that the trip had been neither Aaron's doing nor Cheryl's fault. It was a divine appointment written into my schedule by the hand of God. He had set the time and place. My job was to surrender to what he was telling me.

Saying yes didn't reduce the anxiety one lick. The night before we left, I was still hoping for a last-minute reprieve, longing to hear God say, *This was just a test. Regular programming will now resume.*

By now, my prayer life was reduced to a single word. *Help!* The morning we left, anxiety buckled up in the car right beside me and remained the entire trip.

It's Time to Come Home

We drove with the top down across the sunlit eastern plains of Colorado. Framed by a clear blue sky, the snowcapped Rockies beckoned us onward, guiding us toward our first destination, Colorado Springs, where I was going to deliver a talk on emotional healing to a group of Christian counselors. Reviewing my thoughts helped push aside concerns about California.

As we crested the barren hills east of Colorado Springs, God ambushed me, speaking with the force of divine imperative. I was so startled that I pulled the car onto the dusty side of the road to process what I had just heard.

"Is something wrong? Why did you pull over?"

I looked at Cheryl, surprising myself by the words I was saying. "We have to go to Cedar Springs Hospital. The Lord just told me we have to go there."

"Now?" Cheryl asked. "Are you sure?" And then, "How are you with that?"

I shook my head and answered, "Not good. But that's what I have to do. Pray."

Though I was headed to Colorado Springs for a speaking engagement, it hadn't crossed my mind that the hospital was also located in the Springs. I had thought California would be my Rubicon. But I was wrong.

Instead of being a few days away, the first stop on my healing journey was now just minutes away. Drops of perspiration began to stream from my pores like ants storming out of an anthill. A deep cry kept repeating in my head like the sound of a broken record. *Help me, Jesus. Help me, Jesus.*

When we arrived at the hospital, I was relieved to discover that we weren't allowed to go through the main gates. Instead, we sat down on a wooden bench outside the wrought-iron fence. Though years had passed, the place looked the same. The main building still looked like something out of an old Bela Lugosi movie.

I glanced over at Cheryl, whose warm eyes told me, *It will be okay.* But I wasn't sure I believed her. As I surveyed the campus, I began to play my own version of whack-a-mole, fighting hard to keep old memories from popping their ugly heads to the surface of my mind. In the midst of that impossible game, a memory emerged.

I could see myself standing on the sidewalk the day I'd been admitted. I noticed the agony in my face. My eyes were wet with tears, and my head hung down. Compassion flooded in as I touched a part of myself that had been put away years ago.

In real time I was sitting on a bench outside the gate. But as I allowed myself to be fully present in the memory of that awful day, I could feel the weakness in my legs, the panic in my body, and the loneliness of my broken heart.

A severe grace had carried me across time and space, and for the first time I understood why I had needed to make this journey. It was time to gather up this unrepaired part of myself and take him home.

The man standing paralyzed on the sidewalk, too afraid to enter the hospital but too wounded to turn back, needed to hear the words of hope that only I could bring him. I was there to speak from my experience of healing, which was something he didn't dare dream of. I had come to shout from the housetop that there would be better days, and love, and a greater light that would shine. I was there to comfort his brutally wounded soul, telling him that a new day would be born from the very place where darkness was threatening to tear him apart. I was there to assure him of God's love.

In my heart I cried out, *Lord, don't leave him there. Help me bring that part of myself home once and for all.* I didn't want to spend one more moment suppressing the hellish memory of that hopeless day. Instead, I let myself feel the anxiety and grieve the memory of a loss I had tried to run from. Now it was time to risk touching the heartbreak.

Embracing it, I entered the darkness and voiced to God what I couldn't say back then. *Why, God, why? How could you do this to me? I will forever be a laughingstock, everything lost, all that I have ever done a joke. Do you care? Are you even there? I am dying in a prison of fear, and now this. What will my children think of me? Has anything been real?*

I grieved for myself and for the part of me that stood alone that day. I cried out in the darkness of a place and time in which I felt so little hope. It was the primal scream of my own Gethsemane.

I imagined myself walking toward that man as he shivered on the cold sidewalk. As I walked, I sensed Jesus at my side. Words were few, but love flowed like a river between us. I spoke to the wounded part of myself, saying, *I need you. I want you. I'll never be whole without you. I'm sorry for leaving you behind, but I'm here now and you are coming home with me.* Here in the present, with Christ, I was able to give myself what I had needed such a long time ago. Grief was washed away in the living stream of Holy Presence. I wept with gratitude.

As I wiped the tears from my eyes, I realized that the memory of that day standing outside the hospital no longer had a hold on me. I was free. The anxiety was gone and what remained was peace. On a bench outside a psychiatric hospital in Colorado Springs, a miracle of reclamation happened. The place I had fought so desperately to forget had now become sacred space.

I knew with certainty that it had not been the Lord's anger that had orchestrated this trip across the country but his transforming love.

The Journey Continues

As Cheryl and I continued our journey west, God brought me face to face with other memories. Until then, I hadn't realized the degree to which avoiding the past had kept the unprocessed pain inside me alive. By fighting to silence the evil of yesterday, I had been inviting that same evil into the present day. I was beginning to realize that my daily battles with anxiety had more to do with old memories than with new challenges. Christ's mercy had forced the journey upon me because going back was the answer to moving forward. It wasn't easy, but it was revolutionary.

Now it was time to return to the epicenter of my breakdown, to Redding, California, where I lived in a house behind darkened windows and worked at a church I never wanted to enter again—and a college that showed me the door. At least Aaron and his family were waiting for us there as well.

In spite of my anxiety, God helped me face specific memories in a way that brought healing. Each time, I was able to see myself still trapped emotionally by what had happened. Reexperiencing the memory let me touch the pain, grieve the loss, and integrate that part of my past into my story. That's how I reclaimed the broken parts of myself, welcoming them home. Engaging these episodic memories, in which I was able to reexperience events from my past one by one in the presence of Jesus, was a game changer.

One evening Aaron encouraged the family to join him for a walk along the Sacramento River. The parking lot was empty when we pulled up to the Sundial Bridge. The evening was warm and inviting, a welcome respite from the emotional ups and down I had been experiencing on my healing journey.

As soon as Aaron parked the car, the doors swung open, and the kids spilled out like jelly beans from an overturned jar. Their energy infused life into my spirit. I was looking forward to losing myself in the mesmerizing melody of mountain water rushing to the sea.

Suddenly a van pulled in beside us. Now two vehicles were parked side by side in an ocean of empty spaces. That's when I heard Aaron say, "Oh no!"

As I turned to look, an older man stepped from his car to walk the river trail. Chills ran through my body as goose bumps popped up on my arms. It was a pastor who years before had joined the opposition against me, rallying other pastors and churches and demanding my removal from the college. This was one of the guys who had pushed for a theological examination, and he had made no bones about the fact that he didn't like me one bit.

Now here he was, just steps away and preparing to walk down the same path we had planned to take. I had only one thought. *Not here, not now; let's get in the car and go home.*

But Aaron and the rest of the crew had already taken off down the trail. They moved so quickly I wondered if someone was passing out free ice cream around the next bend. That left me standing at the trailhead alone . . . with *him*!

"Hello, sir, how are you?" he asked. He hadn't recognized me.

Horrible, trapped! That's what I felt like saying. Instead I simply replied, "I'm fine. Lovely evening."

"It is, it is." Then he introduced himself and asked my name.

I paused, extended my hand, and said, "I'm Terry Wardle."

He looked at my face like an accountant double-checking a ledger, sure that something wasn't adding up. Because of his failing eyesight and my receding hairline, it took a few moments for this retired pastor to realize who I was. Then he spoke my name like it was an unwanted reminder of a distant past. "Terry Wardle."

We turned and began to walk the path in silence, side by side. Feeling stuck and bewildered about why this was even happening, I prayed, *What should I do?* and the answer shocked me. *Honor him.*

Honor him? This guy had given me fits. I had things I wanted to tell him straight to his face, but not one of them came close to honoring. And yet the command was clear. *Honor him.*

As we walked across the bridge, the Lord reminded me of the long ministry this man had in the community. Much of his life had been given to making it a better place for everyone. My heart began to soften. Despite our differences, I realized that he was a warrior for the Lord. For that alone he deserved my respect.

I began by thanking him for his faithfulness over the course of many years and asked questions about the ministries he had started, what he had enjoyed most about serving the Lord, and how he was finding retirement. As I did so, God began a work in both our hearts. For the first time, we were talking and getting to know each other. During the space of a few minutes, walls started coming down, and a spark of affection began to grow as an old wound faded. In its place was an experience that would one day become a sweet memory. *Reclamation.*

The Journey Home

Prior to this journey to reclaim parts of myself, I would have characterized my life as one of underlying anxiety with sporadic moments of peace. Though I longed for greater healing, at least I was no longer imprisoned by depression and agoraphobia.

Beneath my outbursts of anger at the prospect of returning to California had been my old enemy, fear. I was scared to death that a return trip would pitch me into a darkness from which I might never emerge. There was loathing, too, because I hated the part of me that was weak, broken, and needy. I would have gladly cut that part out like a surgeon excising a cancerous tumor had I been able. Then I would have stomped on it to make sure it was dead.

My approach couldn't have been more wrongheaded. I could no longer ignore the fact that unprocessed memories take on a life of their own. No matter how deep they are buried, they can produce endless amounts of guilt, shame, anger, and fear.

It shocked me to realize that Jesus loved the parts of me that I despised. Instead of rejecting my past, as I had tried to do, he had reclaimed it. Jesus embraced the weakest parts of my life and infused them with his strength. Suddenly the place of shame held an inheritance I could draw from for the rest of my life.

The journey of reclamation produced a revolution in my soul, a divine turning point that moved me from merely surviving to thriving. I was different after California. It was where I learned to treat the weakest parts of myself as Jesus did, with acceptance, patience, and healing love. I discovered that grace holds no hidden judgment but only transformation. My part was to trust the path God set before me, even when it appeared to lead straight into the painful past.

Fourteen

CRAZY ABOUT YOU

I was attending the Warrior Connection in Raleigh, North Carolina, just moments away from delivering the keynote address. I'd been invited to spend three days with leaders in the black community to focus on what happens to men when society communicates the message that *you don't measure up.*

Our time together felt particularly poignant because a few days earlier, a twenty-one-year-old white supremacist by the name of Dylann Roof walked into the Emmanuel African Methodist Episcopal Church in Charleston, South Carolina, and murdered nine people who had welcomed him into their Bible study.

The men's wives joined us for our final time together. Listening to story after story of deep transformation, I felt undone as I heard strong men weeping about what it had cost them to try to measure up. I listened as those same men spoke about freedom in Christ and what it meant to stand on the solid rock of their identity as children of God.

Just before I stepped up to speak, a man stood up and began walking toward the front. All eyes were on Van as he slowly approached the podium and took hold of the microphone. One of the few white men attending the conference, he began by saying he'd grown up in the Deep South, in a town with a billboard celebrating its identity as the home of the Ku Klux Klan. As Van spoke, people began shifting uncomfortably in their seats. Some dropped their heads while others looked away. He told about growing up where people beat others down as a way of trying to feel better about themselves. As he spoke, he wept.

Then he started talking about what Jesus had done that weekend in his heart. He said he was sorry. He asked for forgiveness. Too choked up to continue, he put the mic down and began the long walk back to his seat through a gauntlet of men and women who'd been severely wounded by the attitudes he had once nurtured in his heart.

What happened next shocked me. As Van approached every row, people left their seats to shake his hand, embrace him, and speak words of gratitude and love. That life march took long moments, but with every passing second, healing love grew in the room. People openly wept. By the time Van made it back to his seat, applause and shouts of praise echoed through the hall. I watched as he fell into his seat, exhausted but remade.

Whatever I had to say after that was irrelevant. God had already spoken. Van's story of transformation made me reflect again on my own long walk to freedom.

You're Not Enough

For forty-three years, my father worked the mines, descending a shaft elevator into the belly of the earth to dig black gold. Day after day he risked his life, making sure we had food on the table and clothes on our backs. For his reward he received black lung disease and an arthritic spine.

My son, Aaron, once asked him if any of his friends had died in the mine. Dad's reply was nonchalant: "Yeah, Bud, the mine took one or two a year at least." While my father cut another piece of cheese to top off his cracker, my son calculated how many deaths that would have been across forty plus years.

I know something about coal mining, too, because I descended the deep shaft twice. The first time was when Dad took me down, and the second was on my first and last day on the job. The work was dangerous and the pay barely enough to make ends meet. For several years my father worked three days one week and two the next.

We ate a lot of ham and cabbage soup and more than our share of navy beans. But once every summer, the coal company rewarded the men with tickets to Kennywood Park for Miners Day. It was the one time we didn't have to endure the embarrassment of standing in food lines at the Presbyterian church, where the county handed out government cheese. At the amusement park, everyone was royalty.

The children of coal miners, my friends and I brought packed lunches of chipped ham sandwiches, potato salad, homemade cupcakes, and ripe watermelons to eat in the park. There was also a lot of Iron City Beer. The men circled up the picnic tables like wagons on the prairie, and kids ran wild. For one day a year, poverty wasn't pulling at the last thread holding their lives together.

There were great rides at Kennywood, including wooden roller coasters named Racer and the Jack Rabbit. There were swimming pools, dance halls, carousels, and cotton candy on every corner. There was also a section called Kiddieland, where I began to hate a national treasure by the name of Howdy Doody.

Howdy Doody was the name of a children's television show starring a wooden marionette of the same name. The puppet sported fire-engine-red hair, ears like flying saucers turned on end, and a huge Polident smile. His face was everywhere—plastered on lunch boxes, sheets, pillowcases, magazine covers, and curtains for a child's bedroom windows.

None of that disturbed me. What turned him into my nemesis was his job at Kennywood.

A Howdy Doody replica, complete with a hideous grin pasted on his sappy face, stood guard outside every good ride. Littered across his painted cheeks were forty-eight orange freckles, each one representing a state. The only way you could get onto the ride was to be as tall as Howdy Doody. Because my gang of friends and cousins was older than I was, they made the cut, while I got left behind. While clambering onto the rides, they would laugh and promise to catch up with me at Kiddieland.

Howdy Doody became another garish symbol of my inability to measure up.

Measuring Up

Known at home as the nervous child or sissy boy and at school as a kid who struggled, I didn't measure up in either of those places. I didn't measure up in church either. Despite my deep experience of God's love as a middle school youth, faith continued to be a strange brew of grace and works. The Lord's grace had saved me, but my performance determined how much of his blessing I might enjoy. Jesus had paid for my sins, but I better not mess things up from there.

Holiness was all about sin management, with the gavel already raised to pronounce judgment at the first sign of my inevitable failure. The church had constructed an ecclesiastical Howdy Doody by teaching that I had to be "this good, this holy, this faithful" to get on God's good side. The fractures in my soul made achieving such ideals impossible, which put me at great risk with the Lord. Instead of being relegated to Kiddieland, I lived in a hinterland of shame.

My insecure, immature faith inevitably led to spiritual neuroticism. Though no one in church admitted it, the underlying formula went like this: Jesus did *almost everything* you need to be secure with God. You are obligated to do the rest. Being right with God was achieved by believing in what Jesus did on the cross and then adding good behavior and sacrificial service. Christians who were able to perform appropriately were on God's A-list. Everyone else who struggled, namely me, was out of luck.

I heard multiple sermons praising the virtues of Real Christians:

- Real Christians have unwavering faith.
- Real Christians resist temptation.
- Real Christians have pure thought lives.
- Real Christians love to read their Bibles.
- Real Christians live clean lives.

And of course the payoff—Real Christians received the best blessings from God.

At almost every level, I violated the standards and failed to measure up as a Real Christian. I wrestled with doubt, at times gave in to temptation, struggled with immoral thoughts, failed to spend every waking moment reading my Bible, and didn't lead the cleanest life.

The Lord and his blessings rested on a high mountain of spiritual maturity. My job was to ascend that mountain through faithful discipleship. When I did, security with the Lord would be mine. But I had an unfortunate problem. A serious emotional limp rendered climbing up that mountain difficult. Even when I made progress, I inevitably slipped up and lost altitude. I did a lot of starting over.

Instead of giving up, I adopted another method, called "try harder." If I was struggling, it was because I hadn't prayed enough, read the Bible enough, gone to church enough, served enough, given enough, or sacrificed enough. If I wanted to be close to Jesus, I had to double down—try twice as hard to reach the high ground where Jesus and real saints hang out.

I kept trying a strategy I called "more." More time in spiritual disciplines, more prayer, more service, more work for the kingdom. If I would clean up my act more, the Lord would be pleased with me, and I could finally live in Christian victory. But performing didn't touch the essential insecurity that nagged at my soul. I still battled fear, still struggled with feeling less than, still didn't measure up. These feelings reinforced the deep sense that there was something fundamentally wrong with me and that nothing would ever change that fact.

The other dilemma was exhaustion. I wore myself out trying to measure up. I worked to be a better Wardle man, went to college to prove I wasn't the family loser, and spent years attempting to become a superpastor. Desperate for solid standing with the Lord, I pressed on to gain the high ground.

The mixture of emotional wounding and performance-driven faith proved deadly. I didn't have the internal capacity for sustained sin management, nor did my efforts ever seem to pay dividends. One day while reading the Gospels, I came across the passage in which Jesus said that following him will bring rest to my soul. *Are you kidding me?* I thought. *Rest? I'm exhausted.*

Jesus's promise that following him would involve an easy yoke seemed as unlikely as stumbling on a palm tree beneath the arctic sun. The Bible says that Jesus welcomes the weary and heavy laden. But the transactional view of Christianity I had embraced, so prevalent in conservative Christian churches, only laid heavier burdens on me. The if-I-do-this-then-God-will-do-that paradigm did nothing to contribute to my healing.

Rather than unleashing me into greater freedom, performance locked me in deeper bondage. No matter how hard I tried to clean myself up I could never rest securely in the peace that was supposed to exist between God and me.

It was only after I had slid down the mountain of "more" that things began to change. Instead of awaiting me at the summit, Jesus, I realized, was standing beside me at the bottom, both of us knee deep in the muck and mire of my woundedness. It was there that he was touching me with his love. He hadn't waited until I cleaned myself up because he knew I couldn't clean myself up. Instead, he cleaned me up *as* he was loving me. I didn't have to earn, perform, or achieve. All I had to do to be secure with him was say yes to his all-transforming, forever-securing, freely given, crazy love.

A Window of the Soul

One day Aaron called to tell me that Destry had been diagnosed with preeclampsia and rushed by ambulance to the hospital. Her symptoms were escalating despite the fact that doctors were frantically working to lower her blood pressure.

Like people hailing cabs in the middle of New York City, we started contacting prayer warriors across the country, asking them to pray that the Lord would do what he does best—help!

At one point, when Aaron was close to exhaustion and walking the hallways begging God to intervene, a janitor heard him mumbling under his breath. "Can I help you, young man?" she asked.

"I'm just praying, ma'am. My wife is about to have a baby, and it isn't going so well. I'm kinda afraid here, so I'm talking to Jesus."

"Oh my," she said. "Don't you get me talkin' 'bout my Jesus."

That dear unnamed saint showed up like an angel of God dressed in a janitorial jumpsuit. She encouraged Aaron, told stories of how Jesus had saved her life and family, and then prayed, all the while holding her mop and bucket like they were the rod and staff of Christ himself. Aaron found solid ground right beside the sign that read "Slippery when wet."

Since medication wasn't helping Destry, her physicians opted for surgery. In mere minutes systems were go, and the baby we had all been waiting for arrived. More than two months early, she weighed less than two pounds and needed constant attention so she could have a fighting chance.

Gaining visitor access to the neonatal intensive-care unit of that hospital seemed more difficult than going through the front gate at the White House. But we knew the medical staff was fighting for the baby's life. Once inside, Cheryl and I looked into the incubator, peering at our granddaughter. She was tiny and needed constant care, with tubes attached at the top of her head. It would be weeks, perhaps months, before she could come home. Despite her immaturity, weakness, and neediness, we welcomed her as a 100 percent member of the Wardle family—a Real Wardle.

The baby didn't have to get healthy, develop, perform, or please us in order to become a Real Wardle. She was already secure as our cherished granddaughter no matter what might happen.

In the years that have followed, she's grown into a beauty, a star athlete, a great student, a talented guitarist, and a girl who gives her grandparents the impression she is nuts about them. But none of what she has become has added to her rock-solid status as a Wardle. Her membership in our tribe is not about maturity. Whatever happens, she will always be part of our family. That's the nature of grace, which, by the way, happens to be the name her parents gave her.

Grace Wardle is, and always will be, a Real Wardle.

"Grace My Fears Relieved"

Like Grace, I had joined God's family not in a moment of strength but in a time of weakness. Though it had taken me years, I finally understood that my security is not based on my behavior but is a gift of grace.

When Jesus embraced me in the dirtiest places of my tangled past, I started to understand the scandal of outrageous love. Rather than demanding I ascend to it, love came down to me. I discovered that love gave, love hoped, love believed, love transformed, even when I couldn't respond. Love didn't judge or condemn or lay out impossible performance expectations as the prerequisite of blessing. Love crossed the universe and gave up life to give me life.

Touched by transforming love, I wanted to know Jesus more. More was available because I was part of the family. It didn't depend on whether I prayed more, read more, gave more, or served more. It was mine as part of my inheritance as God's child. There was nothing I could add to what Jesus had already done for me.

The formula of grace was far different from what I had been taught. It wasn't true that Jesus has done *almost everything* I needed to be secure in my relationship with God. He has done *everything,* which meant I could add absolutely nothing. No Jesus plus. No rules that must be followed to unleash the Father's blessings. The promises of God were mine because of Christ, not because of me.

The teachings of Scripture came alive. How many times had I read, "It is for freedom that Christ has set us free" without understanding what that meant? I no longer needed to try to measure up to all the rules, rituals, and religious obligations people said were necessary to be secure with God. Even more liberating was the realization that performance compromised rather than enhanced my relationship with Jesus.

I could see it. I could feel it. I knew it—that crazy, scandalous, life-changing, I-will-never-again-be-the-same kind of love that is God's love. I was his child by grace, filled with the Spirit by grace, and given an inheritance, once again by grace. Jesus had lived the perfect life and then assigned the benefits to me. All I had to do was believe and receive. I was getting addicted to Jesus, and it was wonderful.

The story Jesus told about the prodigal son began to take on a new light. Thinking it a tale of sin and repentance, I had preached sermons detailing how the prodigal had "come to his senses," admonishing people to do the same. As I read it again, with a fresh sense of who I am in Christ, the Spirit revealed that it was fundamentally a parable about having security with the Father. It was a lesson on what it meant to have my identity rooted in being a child of God.

I sensed the Lord guiding me through the story by asking specific questions about the son.

What was true of the prodigal before he wandered away? asked Jesus.

I answered, *He was the father's son.*

What was true of the prodigal even while he was far away squandering his inheritance?

He was the father's son.

When he returned, what was the first thing the father wanted the prodigal to know? Even after he had wasted the father's money, stepped away from the father's love, and compromised his own health and well-being in the process? As the prodigal stood there reeking from too many lunches with hogs, what did the father want his prodigal child to know?

The answer was breathtaking: *He was the father's son.*

The prodigal's father was so intent on securing his son's identity that he brought rings and robes and a fatted calf to reaffirm what was forever true. "Even after all this, you are my child! You were before you left. You were while you were gone. And you are as you stand here today. On both your best day and your worst day, you belong with me."

The scandal of grace captured my heart and wouldn't let me go.

For most of my life, I had worked hard to change my behavior in order to be accepted by God. It had never worked. But now I knew that God's love did work. Jesus taught me that I had always been secure in my identity as God's child. From the moment I opened my heart to him years earlier, all the benefits of the kingdom had been mine. They were mine when I was in the ditch, mine when I struggled with faith, mine when I made mistakes, mine even though I felt I wasn't measuring up. How could I explain such lavish grace except to conclude that God was crazy about me?

One day while speaking at a seminar, I asked the audience a series of simple questions. It was great fun seeing eyes and hearts open up to the reality of all Christ had done for them. I asked:

"Is there anyone here who is sure they are going to heaven?" People said yes.

"How did that happen?" There was a brief pause, and then someone said, "Jesus."

"Does anyone here have the Holy Spirit living inside?" Some folks said yes.

"How did you get that to happen?" The answer was again, "Jesus."

"Is there anyone here who has spiritual gifts?" Several people answered yes.

"How did you get those gifts?" Another pause followed, and then someone said, "Jesus."

On and on I went. I listed blessing after blessing, and whenever I asked how that happened, the answer was always the same: "Jesus." Not once did performance, or measuring up, or working harder, or praying more ever get spoken. We were affirming the truth of the

Bible, which says, "For no matter how many promises God has made, they are 'Yes' in Christ" (2 Corinthians 1:20).

My confidence as a follower of Christ rested in this—that I am my Father's son. That was the unshakable certainty of my identity, the foundation of what it meant to be loved, accepted, delighted in, and significant. Even my mess could never change that fact. It was then I realized that no one gets to define me but Jesus. Not even me.

The wonder of healing love, the security of my identity in Christ, and the generous promises of God initiated a new paradigm for my spiritual growth. Instead of striving to change *in order* to be secure, I *positioned* myself for transformation because I was secure.

I went to Scripture, not to earn points for good behavior, but to position myself to meet Jesus. I prayed, not as evidence of my Christian maturity, but because God shows up there. I served, not to prove my value as a Christian, but out of the overflow of abundant love.

One day Cheryl and I passed a billboard on the highway that read, "Real Christians obey the teachings of Christ." Some well-intentioned believer had invested a lot of money in that sign, wanting to call Christ followers to maturity in Jesus. But the inherent flaw in the message saddened me. It screamed performance. It said to the world that the one thing that establishes relationship with God is how you behave. To be "real" a person had to be obedient.

Had the sign read, "Real Christians would do well to obey the teachings of Christ," I could have said "amen." Or "Real Christians should grow up to obey the teachings of Christ" or "Real Christians would be smart if they asked the Spirit to help them obey the teachings of Christ," again, I would have had no problem. I knew that people become children of God the moment they surrender to Christ's embrace.

As I continued to stumble down the path that leads from broken to beloved, I knew the crazy truth—that I was a Real Christian from the top of my head all the way down to the tips of my toes.

Fifteen

BY WHAT RIGHT?

Cheryl and I were leaving for Richmond, where I was scheduled to speak at a retirement celebration for a pastor who'd been a longtime friend. As I was about to close the suitcase, she smiled and handed me a package. It was a new shirt to wear for the Sunday service, a high-end white number to be worn with the only matching pair of cuff links I could fish out of my sock drawer. The shirt cost more than the suit I'd packed.

Cheryl said she had only one request. I thought it might be about remembering to wash my farmer's neck or waiting to eat until after I preached, since I was famous for wearing lunch on my shirt.

"Terry, please don't take your fountain pen. You know how it leaks, and this is an expensive shirt. Okay?"

"Got it!" Enough said.

The event went well and several people even complimented my appearance. I felt buoyed by their warm response. As I mingled at the reception that followed, a person asked, "What is the logo on your shirt?"

"Oh, there is a logo?" I said, opening my suit coat to see for myself. One look at my shirt left me feeling suddenly sick—as though I were battling the flu, and I was the swine. I had disobeyed, broken the rule, crossed the line, gone way out of bounds. Despite promising Cheryl I would not bring my fountain pen, I had tucked it into my coat pocket. Exactly as prophesied, the lid had fallen off and the ink had leaked through my suit coat onto my new shirt. My designer-logo stain was located below the left pocket—about the size of Ethiopia and as black as tar. I stared in guilty disbelief.

Though I felt lifted up by the service, I slid all the way down to a shame-filled funk because of my Rorschach-inspired attire. There was no hiding my mistake unless I stripped off the shirt and threw it in the trash. The thought was tempting, but when I envisioned the response from the folks at the reception, I discarded the idea as impractical. Buttoning my suit coat, I set out to find Cheryl.

Crawling toward her like a whipped puppy, I barked out several mea culpas while pointing to Exhibit A. Then I apologized at least a hundred times. With earnestness.

Instead of rolling her eyes in disgust, Cheryl grinned as though to tell me she was not a bit surprised. Kissing me on the cheek, she assured me all was forgiven. Then she suggested I keep the shirt and simply wear it under a sweater or vest. But I resisted, sure it would forever remind me of my guilty deed. It deserved the burn pile as penance. After all, I knew something about such fires!

Forgiveness Growing Up

In my parent's home, mistakes were never met with kindness. Nor were they ever forgotten, perhaps because they made such handy emotional hammers, driving home the message that I had better straighten up or else.

When people in my world did forgive an offense, they did so by "gunnysacking." A gunnysack is a cheap burlap bag with a drawstring, used to hold rusted and broken odds and ends that a person might find useful sometime in the future. Gunnysacking emotionally meant extending temporary and conditional forgiveness, with the accompanying threat that whatever had previously happened could be pulled out anytime and anyplace to remind me of how I had failed in the past, ammunition of sorts to insure the upper hand in a touch and go dispute.

Some in my tribe shouldered gunnysacks the size of freight cars, with more than a few relatives picking up an offense and carrying it all the way to the grave. One of my cousins made the mistake of marrying a woman his dad disliked. After being told he should never come home with her again, he stayed away for more than fifty years.

My mother was raised with several cousins who were as close to her as brothers. Each were in our home almost daily as I grew up and were treated as members of our immediate family. However, when one of them made a disparaging comment about her uncle, Mom let him have it, stating that he was nothing but a pain in her posterior. Though they had been thick as thieves for decades, and though both were in their late seventies, my mother and cousin never spoke again.

By What Right?

What a contrast it was to have someone in my life like Cheryl, who had learned to extend forgiveness so generously, with no strings attached. Her generous love spoke volumes about God's kindness.

One day I was invited to speak on emotional trauma to counseling students at a regional theological seminary. As was often the case, I shared openly about my own wounded past. Though my audience warmed to the message, I wasn't prepared for a question asked by a faculty member.

"Dr. Wardle, with all due respect, what qualifies you to speak about counseling and emotional healing?"

Assuming she was inquiring about my academic background, I answered by talking about my education, internships, degrees, and experience.

"That's not what I meant," she said. "We all heard your story, and well, I am asking a question related to your personal journey and the choice to help people who are struggling psychologically."

I appreciated her clarification and began talking about my experience receiving therapy and spiritual direction. I spoke of the deep changes that had occurred in my life over the years. But none of that satisfied her.

"Allow me to be more blunt," she said. "Your story is one of mistakes, sin, weakness, even mental illness. By what right do you talk to other people about their Christian journey when it appears you have made such a mess of your own?"

The question hung heavily in the room as people cleared their throats and looked down at their shoes.

"I have asked myself that question more times than I can count," I began. "Why me? There are far better Christians than I and most certainly far healthier ones. I have sat up nights worrying about this very thing. Great question."

The truth was that I had battled diagnosable psychological problems for years and had blown it more times than most people could count. Whatever lessons I had learned came more from failure than success. Like Scrooge poring over his finances, I had often mulled the ledger of my misdeeds.

Preoccupied

If my life were a tapestry, it would include too many knotted threads where the brokenness of sin and wounding had compromised what might otherwise have been an acceptable weave. In one sense, it was right to be dissatisfied with all that had happened. I had needed to repent. My sin and brokenness were clear evidence of why I desperately needed a Savior.

But I had learned that obsessing over my broken past never motivated me to run from sin. It only made me miserable. Wallowing in the quicksand of regret would drive me toward self-contempt, keeping my eyes forever on myself. Instead of focusing on my failure, my sorrow had driven me toward the tenderness of Christ.

I remembered the story in the Gospels about the Pharisee who criticized the woman washing Jesus's feet with her hair. He could see only her sinfulness. But Jesus saw her love, which he had linked to the magnitude of his forgiveness. Because she was forgiven much, she loved much.

Instead of sin driving me toward deeper regret, it became the birthplace for great love and devotion. Ignatius of Loyola's words rang true in my heart: "All I can do is give thanks to him that, up to this moment, has shown himself so loving and merciful to me." Rather than tallying the wrongs I had done in my life, I became preoccupied with the joy of his amazing forgiveness.

Because of the way God had forgiven me, I felt free. Even though I might be the "worst of sinners," I was still God's son. It was the generosity of Christ that made me long to serve him by serving others. His love and acceptance was what had given me the right to talk to broken people about healing.

A Wounded Healer

Something else helped me accept the ministry the Lord had given me. It was the notion of being a "wounded healer," a phrase coined by Henri Nouwen. His central premise was that weaknesses and wounds touched by Christ actually become the locus of the most effective ministry you can offer others.

Despite the emphasis on performance in the conservative Christian communities that had nurtured my faith, I learned that wounds did serve healing. People listened more, not less, when they knew I had spent time in the ditch. It didn't take much reflection to realize that the church had a long tradition of celebrating the wounds of Jesus, understanding that these brought healing. Christ's power was being perfected in my weakness.

Most of those who attended my seminars were drawn not by my educational credentials but because they knew I had met Jesus in a place of weakness. They were ready to embrace my experience as a pathway to grace for their own lives. The wounded-healer paradigm linked Christ to their own stories.

Many people have thanked me for being honest about my mess because it gives them permission to be honest about their own. One man asked if I was in fact healed. I smiled and said, "Yes, I am healed, I am being healed, and I am yet to be healed." That answer gave him hope for the journey.

I didn't have time to explain all this to the faculty person who had challenged my credentials. But I did tell her that part of what made God so amazing was that he had lavishly gifted a person like me. Reducing my explanation even further, I offered a one-word explanation: Grace, it was all grace.

The Sacramento

My understanding of forgiveness hadn't always been so complete. One morning I had a profound experience with the Lord. The Holy

Spirit created a picture in my mind of me standing beside the Sacramento River in Redding. I was on the eastern bank where the river turns south with violent force on its own journey toward the sea. I felt the mist-filled wind as it blew across my face, heard the water rushing by, and saw the sun reflecting off the rough water at my feet.

Suddenly, in a moment of prophetic imagination, I looked to my right, and there stood Jesus on the bank beside me. His eyes radiated love, and his Presence brought me a peace that refreshed my soul.

As I gazed at him, I noticed his arms were filled. He seemed to be carrying all the brokenness and sin of my life. Every mistake, each act of disobedience, was held by the Lord as though he were carrying the weight of my failure on his body. Looking at me with a radiant face of acceptance and love, he tossed my broken past into the river, and then said, *I love you this much.*

I watched as every object of shame was washed downstream and then swept out of sight. It was a profound moment of grace. As I looked at Christ through tears of gratitude, he said, *Isn't it time you empty what you have been carrying in your arms and forgive him?* The "him" was my dad.

Why the Forgiven Forgive

Like my mother, Dad had left a trail of deep wounding in my life. His emotional abandonment and scorn had set me up for a lifelong battle with low self-esteem. While other men had invested in me during my teenage years, he had little to do with me. His unspoken disdain had colored our relationship for years.

As a Christian man, I had worked hard to let go of my resentment, and over time we began to grow closer. God's grace was at work in us both. But recent decisions had brought old wounds to life again.

As I imagined myself standing on the banks of the Sacramento, I realized that Jesus was challenging a silent grudge that had formed in my heart.

Dad had always promised me his shotguns and rifles. When I was young, I would gaze through the glass gun case, imagining the day when they would be mine. Though there weren't many and none were expensive collectibles, those guns connected me, for better or worse, to men who had shaped my understanding of masculinity. One had even belonged to Uncle Fat.

Dad said he would give me his tools too. He had chests and cabinets filled with wrenches, pliers, cutters, screwdrivers, and a vast array of gizmos and gadgets he had collected over the years. I loved the feel of cold steel in my hands and was grateful Dad was willing to pass them along to me. It made me feel special to think he had thought of me, especially since his own father had left him nothing.

But when my parents sold their house to move into assisted living, Dad gave away half his guns to a couple of relatives. Then he gave another relative first choice on half his tools. I was surprised and disappointed. It wasn't about guns or tools but about not being valued. When I spoke to him about it later, I received little more than an "oops."

Now, as I saw myself standing on the edge of the Sacramento, I thought about Jesus opening his arms and letting go of all my sins. Touching that joy enabled me to extend the same forgiveness to Dad.

Afterward, I realized there is a flow to the generosity of God. As he gave to me, I was moved to give to Dad. Releasing my father released me. That must have been why Jesus instructed Peter to forgive not seven times but seventy-seven times. Forgiveness does more than clean a slate. It empowers joy.

Cleansing

Two weeks after returning home from Richmond, Cheryl walked into the house carrying clothes she'd picked up at the cleaners.

"Look," she said with a smile. "It's clean!"

She was holding the white shirt I'd ruined, and it didn't have a mark on it. I stared in disbelief, first, because I thought I had thrown it away and, second, because it looked brand-new.

"How in the world . . . is that my shirt?"

"It is. I took it to the cleaners and told them about what happened. I'm not sure how they did it, but look, you can't even see the shadow of where that stain was."

I was more touched than when Cheryl first gave me the shirt. The fact that she wouldn't give up, even after I had, took the expression of her love and forgiveness to an entirely new level. She had paid for the shirt. When I blew it, she forgave me. Finally, she worked to make my mistake go away so I never had to look at the mess I had made. It almost sounded biblical.

Sixteen

WHY ARE YOU SO AFRAID?

The atmosphere was electric. The two hundred people who had gathered for a leadership event seemed ready for a party, waiting for God to break in at any moment and do his stuff. I could sense that many in the room were expecting an outpouring of the Holy Spirit, looking, as one participant put it, "for God to show up and show off!" We all wanted more of Jesus.

I spoke on my favorite topic, the matchless love of God. Moved by the crowd and the Spirit, I passionately drilled down on the fact that we are loved in spite of our brokenness, welcomed even in our woundedness, and secure as God's children even when our behavior does not reflect who we are in Christ.

Smiles, tears, nodding heads, and raised hands told me the message was hitting home. God was in the room, and the debilitating spirit of performance was being exposed for what it was and then broken. What could be shaken was being shaken, and we were the better for it.

Sharing the message of scandalous grace impacted me as much as it did my audience. The more I declared God's expansive love, the deeper it soaked into my soul. This was so even though I didn't yet speak the language of grace fluently. Like a blind man suddenly given sight, I was experiencing faith in ways I had not known, and it was stunning.

As the evening drew to a close, I felt the best kind of exhaustion, undone from swimming in a sea of God's transforming love. I made my way through the crowd and found myself inhabiting the space between deep gratitude and pure exhilaration, humbled that I could be part of such a breakthrough moment.

I had almost reached the door when I felt a hand forcefully pull me around. There stood a woman looking at me as if I were the devil himself. "So I have a question for you," her lips snarled in contempt. "God loves me no matter what, does he? Well, do you think he will love me when I let him have it? When I tell him exactly how much he has disappointed me? Will he delight in me then?"

I stuttered out an answer, but she wasn't having it.

"I've been shoving down anger at God for years. I've worked hard to be a good little soldier. Say the right thing, do the right thing, play nice. After all, he holds all the chips, doesn't he? Play by his rules or else. All you did tonight, with all this he-loves-you-no-matter-what nonsense, was unleash the ugliest part of me because, frankly,

God ripped me off, and I've been living with the pain ever since. Does he love me enough to hear that?"

Shaken by her reproach, I squeaked out a response. "Yes. God loves you even that much."

"We'll see," she said. She turned and pushed her way out the door, parting the crowd as efficiently as Moses had the Red Sea.

Waves of embarrassment, disappointment, and anger nearly knocked me off my feet. All through the night questions pressed down on me like a giant steamroller. *Did I just make a mess for someone? Was my response to her true? Could she be safe if she was gut-level honest with God? Did the Lord love her that much? Or was Mom right when she said that heads would roll?*

That confrontation would soon ignite the most honest conversation I ever had with God. Her angry questions had given me permission to face into my own disappointments, and when they surfaced it was volcanic.

No Holds Barred

"You know that place between sleep and awake, that place where you still remember dreaming? That's where I'll always love you. That's where I'll be waiting." These words from the screenplay for *Hook* struck a chord with me because the space between asleep and awake had never offered me that kind of hope. Instead, it was a dreaded unlit world, the breeding ground of despair brought on by unhealed wounds. In that smoky haze of not yet awake, I would startle from another violent dream, my covers twisted as tight as the knot in my stomach. As I struggled to push through to consciousness, my heart would pound out of my chest while I tried to determine what was real and what was merely another ugly nightmare tearing at my soul.

Tossing aside the jumble of covers, I wanted to scream from pent-up frustration. Would the torture ever stop? Surges of adrenaline would leave my mind in a fog and make me wonder whether I was about to press my face through the thin veil separating sanity from insanity. Though I wanted to run, there was never anywhere to go.

On more normal days I arose early to meet the Lord in predawn solitude. A favorite chair was sacred space, Bible and journal close at hand. The stillness of long seasons in quiet prayer was a sanctuary for my soul, the place to search for the One I always found searching for me.

Not so when morning panic grabbed me by the throat. Too anxious to sit, too angry to wait, I found that the thought of prayer usually gave birth to resentment. *Where was God?* I hated whatever made me lean so easily toward fear.

One morning, desperate from another restless awakening, I tried to read the Bible to calm my fears. When I did, my anger built to volcanic proportions. The day's reading focused on the story of Jesus being asleep in the boat as his disciples fought for their lives. *Perfect,* I thought. *That was exactly how I felt. Jesus was nodding off at the precise moment I was going under!*

What most infuriated me about the passage was the way Jesus responded when his disciples woke him up. These crazy Christ followers were afraid of dying, and Jesus faith-shamed them. "You of little faith," he chided. What kind of response was that when someone was trying to save his life? It seemed beyond insensitive. It was mean. Then Jesus had the nerve to ask a question to which the answer seemed painfully obvious. "Why are you so afraid?" The disciples said nothing. Had I been there, Jesus would have gotten an earful.

"Why am I afraid, Jesus?" I would have asked. *"First, I don't appreciate you coming down on me at a time like this. I woke you up because I was afraid for you as well. Instead of thanking me, you question my spiritual manhood. I'll tell you why else I'm afraid. An angry storm is pounding against this small boat, and if the waves persist, it's going down. When it does, so does my livelihood. If this boat sinks, so does my chance at feeding my family. And you wonder why I am afraid?*

"Oh, and as a side note, Jesus, I don't swim too well, so if I'm thrown into the water, I won't last long. Instead of returning home to people I love, I'll end up sucking water into my lungs, becoming chum bait for every passing fish. You ask me why I'm afraid. Are you joking? Please tell me you're not that clueless."

Things Get Real, Fast

I was blinded by rage that morning, unwilling to play nice with God any longer. It wasn't enough to know that Jesus would eventually still the storm. I'd had enough bad weather for ten lifetimes. Though I'd begged God for freedom, he'd thrown a Bible lesson in my face instead.

I paced the floor, caught up in my own jaded view of reality. Then a thought took shape in my mind. Given my years-long struggle with an anxiety disorder and countless hours spent pleading with God for relief, was it so surprising that the question Why are you so afraid? infuriated me? I didn't even dare address the anger I felt about the "you of little faith" comment.

Even had I wanted to adopt a more respectful posture, I couldn't. I was too far gone for that. That's when the question turned personal, and I thought I heard Jesus ask: *Why are you so afraid?*

Are you serious, Jesus? You're asking me? I have spent a lifetime asking you that same question, but now it's on me? Well, ready or not, here it comes! The gloves are off because I refuse to play nice one more second.

With that, I went for it, telling Jesus the truth about how I felt. It wasn't pretty, but it felt good.

Maybe I battle fear because my pregnant mother said daily that she couldn't wait to get the baby out of her because she was so afraid of giving birth. Do you think that could have affected me? I should have been safe in my mother's womb instead of swimming in an ocean of her fear.

Or what about the fact that before I could walk I went into shock from the excruciating pain of boiling water being poured on my face and chest? Grandma Til had slipped and scalded me when I was cuddling up behind her. Afterward she insisted that no one ever speak about what had happened. I would never have known about it had I not asked Mom about the scars on my face when I was a teenager.

Is it possible that these ridiculously uncaring, unprotected moments made me a fearful person, made it tough for me to trust people? Could they have embedded fear into every cell of my body?

I have cried out, "Why am I so afraid?" ten thousand times across the years. Did it start when my grandfather abused me as a child, or how about my mother's inability to attach, or the unpredictable outbursts of meanness and punishment from both my parents?

Or how about the day my father chased me through my grandmother's backyard in a screaming rage, beating me for throwing a stone? After that I was a five-year-old who couldn't even lower himself into the tub because of bruises to his backside. All because I had to pay the freight for frustrations regarding his life and marriage. Any seed of fear planted there?

What about cowering in my room, alone and sick, hoping in vain that Mom wouldn't find out and apply her favorite remedy? What about Dad walking by and doing nothing as I lay on the bathroom floor?

I was only five years old when my grandfather suffered a hideous death less than ten feet from where I stood. I can still touch the terror that flooded over me night after night, when I was unable to breathe because of the grip that panic had on me. I was afraid to close my eyes for fear I would die in my sleep.

I was six when Great-Grandma Murdy died in the middle of the night in the bed right next to mine. I heard Grandma Mose cry out in the dark, "My God, Mum's dead!" I watched as adults cried uncontrollably at the bed beside me. I was a kid, Jesus, just a kid. Please, tell me, was that where it started? Because I want to know.

Or what about my mother's nightly ritual? Chairs were forced under every doorknob, double and triple locks were checked and re-checked as my sister and I listened to Mom's incessant warnings that bad people wanted to get into the house and "knock us all on the head."

By the way, Lord, you're not off the hook either. Mom told me you would knock my face off if I wasn't a good boy. I learned a lot about hell but not much about heaven. She said that bad children got lumps of coal in their Christmas stockings, and in her version the coal was on fire! Even the word "God" brought on a rush of fear whenever I heard it. That's right, Lord. You scared me to death. How deep do those wounds go, Lord? And you still ask, "Why are you afraid?"

Jesus, on days like this, when fear rises up in that dreaded space between awake and asleep, when I can't shake the foreboding that threatens to undo me before the day has even begun, I question if anything will ever change. I don't need one more lesson in theology. So why did you even ask the question, Why are you so afraid?

"You of Little Faith"

My harangue that morning lacked the necessary respect and theological sophistication most Christians expect. But my words were honest, reflecting the angst that had built up because of the fear that had been planted inside me since boyhood.

As I continued to wrestle with God, I began to wonder if I had misunderstood the "little faith" statement Jesus had made to his disciples. What if he wasn't chiding them but saying something quite different? What if he was telling them that sometimes in life there are big issues that "little faith" can't touch?

Maybe "little faith" works for a parking space at the mall or extra cash to get you through to the next paycheck or an answer on a test. But could Jesus have been saying tough times demand tougher faith?

Hope began to break through my desolation. Maybe the Lord was agreeing that my battle with fear was a big deal, not easily walked out, not quickly resolved. I began to experience relief as I realized that Jesus understood my frustration and seemed to be validating the intensity of the fight. I could breathe again.

Maybe some battles demand "big faith." But now the question was, What is big faith? Is it a throw-that-mountain-into-the-sea kind of faith or a no-shadow-of-a-doubt form of belief? Is it the certainty that no matter the storm, Jesus will calm the sea, steady my boat, heal every disease, and make me leap over tall buildings in a single bound?

By now my emotions were ragged-edge raw. But what I had heard from the Lord while wrestling with the story that morning brought an entirely new perspective to my understanding of faith. At one level, what I had perceived from Christ undid me; at another, it pressed me more deeply into an intimate dependence upon him.

The Holy Spirit drew me back to the story, reminding me how I had said that I would have been terrified of drowning in the boiling sea. That's when Jesus spoke into my heart. He said there were two ways he could intervene. He could save me. Door number one! Full deliverance, no harm, all is well. The other, far less appealing option was that I could perish—but he would still be there with me.

Jesus seemed to be saying that he was able to deliver me from my fear or be with me even when my fear did not subside. But wait. Was being at peace about the possibility of not being healed really an expression of faith? Doesn't faith mean I'm trusting in full deliverance at the hand of Jesus?

As I posed those questions, I was surprised by the response I received. "Little faith" insists that Jesus always calm the storm, heal the disease, eliminate all the fear from my life. This is good faith, necessary faith, even miracle-working faith. But Jesus seemed to be saying that "big faith" takes trust to an entirely new level.

Big faith recognizes that two options are present in every trial. There is the possibility of complete deliverance as Jesus calms the sea. But there is also the option of trusting him even when the storm doesn't subside. For me that translated into trusting him whether he completely healed my anxiety or not.

Big faith is when I look to Christ and say, "Jesus, you choose." Big faith is the ability to relinquish my desire and submit to what the Lord deems necessary, knowing that his love always chooses what's best whether or not I understand what he's doing.

The only phrase that came close to representing this level of faith was "Not my will, but yours be done," or as Job said, "Though he slay me, yet I will hope in him."

As the light broke through in my clouded mind, I had nothing more to say. I still longed for complete freedom, but for the first time I understood that some situations in my life demanded big faith. I needed to surrender to the Lord and honestly say, "You choose."

That morning delivered two certainties. First, I knew that I didn't yet have big faith. Second, beneath my desire for complete healing lay a deeper longing. I wanted to be so at rest in the love of God that I would be able to say in the midst of my struggles, "You choose the outcome, Lord." I wanted to embrace the truth that though we are not always healed, we are always held by him.

My prayer that morning was that Jesus would transform that dreaded space between asleep and awake. That I would sense him waiting for me in the place where I still remembered dreaming and that's where he would always love me.

I had no idea that my struggle to understand the difference between little faith and big faith would be the grand prelude to a great testing in my life. Soon I would awaken in a place that demanded a level of trust in God I did not have.

Seventeen

SOMETHING IN THIS TROUBLE

I chuckled as soon as I caught sight of him, a complete stranger who could have been my doppelganger. Dressed in the exact outfit I was wearing—a gray cardigan, black crewneck shirt, and black jeans, he even wore glasses like mine. This was an opportunity too good to pass up.

Each day of the seminar had begun with my handing out random gifts—to the people who had driven the farthest, had a birthday closest in time, were married the longest, and so on. It was a fun way to set a lighthearted tone, especially since the seminar focused on trauma and emotional healing. Now I had found another category to reward.

"Folks," I said, "I have a special prize to start the day." I reached behind to my collection of books and selected one I thought especially nice.

"Today I am going to give away this great big, really expensive book to the person in the room that looks most like me." People laughed, looked at each other, pointed across the room, and enjoyed the fun. I walked back and forth across the platform surveying the crowd. "So let me see . . . hmm . . . no . . . not you . . . kinda close. Not you, either, though I like that shirt you're wearing. There, right there. You, sir. Come up here because you win the prize."

As the man came forward, the audience howled with laughter. After about six or seven steps, he stopped in his tracks, looked at me, looked at himself, and then started to laugh himself.

Apparently that connection emboldened him because after the day ended, he asked to talk. Steve and I found a table in the corner and sat down. "Terry, I just had to say something to you. I've been to a couple of seminars you did some years back. There is something different about you now. I mean, you seem, I don't know, more at ease. It's like there is a peace about you I hadn't seen before. I wanted to tell you that. You kinda turned into a gentle guy or something, and it's, well, great."

"Thanks, Steve," I replied. And then, "That means the world to me. Like the song says, 'It's no secret what God can do.' "

"I get that," he said. "But it feels like you ended up in a really good space. It showed this week, and I wanted you to know that."

What Steve couldn't have known was how hard it had been to get to that "really good space." I had to be kicked out of where I was in life in order to step into the will of God.

Can You Drink This Cup?

The leg of the journey began with a bang. After more than two decades teaching at the seminary and after developing a healing ministry that had brought thousands of people onto the campus, I was told to find another location to help broken people find healing. My assistant was also being let go as a result of the decision. The new administration didn't share my vision for emotional healing or the emphasis I placed on kingdom theology. I was told that the institute I had founded on campus would be shut down to make room for a new initiative more in line with the new leadership's progressive agenda. I wondered if this was about control and power more than theology. Regardless, I was invited out.

The announcement was both confusing and heartbreaking. When I asked about the reasons behind the decision, misrepresentations regarding the impact and breadth of my ministry followed. My efforts to clarify were met with more tension and an ever-broadening narrative inconsistent with what I knew to be true. It didn't take long for me to get the point—that it was a new day at the seminary and that neither I nor the ministry I had started was welcome.

The decision threw me into a tailspin. For three months I twisted in knots, beating on doors to get a hearing. But nothing changed. I had entered an alternate universe where up was down, no was yes, and simple Christian charity was in short supply.

I had been here twice before in my ministry, and the thought of a third trip into heartache and disappointment did not sit well. The voices of rejection from my time in Nyack began to taunt me in the night. The faces of those who opposed me in Redding began to reappear in my thoughts. Was this to be, in the immortal words of Yogi Berra, "Déjà vu all over again"?

In the middle of these frustrations, I awoke one night at three a.m. and then headed down to my study to pray. So much of what I was facing was simply not right. I believed it was a spiritual attack, as did a few of my closest friends. I let the Lord know what I thought, hoping for much-needed help. But my prayers felt about as life giving as breathing through an old army gas mask. Long on effort, short on respiration.

Then the Lord spoke an unwelcome word into my heart. Unmistakably from Jesus, it was quite unappreciated on my end. I was fighting the forces of darkness in prayer, calling for God's army to come down and scorch the earth, asking for the waters to part, rivers to rise, and the four horsemen of the apocalypse to mount up with shield and buckler to save the day. In response I sensed Jesus asking, *Can you drink this cup?*

Drink this cup? Who was talking about taking communion? Didn't the Lord know there was a threat heading my way and, more importantly, to the ministry he had commissioned? Drink this cup?

I felt more than a little stumped. After all, drink-this-cup statements in the Bible never seemed to turn out well for the person doing the drinking. Whenever it came up it seemed that crucifixion and death soon followed. What did being booted from the seminary have to do with that? Yet when I asked the Lord, he repeated the question.

Can you drink this cup?

There I was, in the middle of the night, asking for divine intervention, and all of a sudden things were turning . . . on me. What I said next is embarrassing.

Lord, do you have any idea how hard it is to have people say things about you that aren't true? To have someone stomp all over your ministry while a bunch of people you thought were friends stand around and . . . Oh.

I gave a nervous chuckle and apologized. I think Jesus laughed as well and then asked me again: *Can you drink this cup?*

I was beginning to catch on. Maybe there was something in this trouble I needed. If I were willing to "drink this cup," something in these difficulties would form me. Rather than fighting against what was occurring, I was to be shaped through it. I was to find Jesus in the darkness and say yes to the transformation he would bring. It seemed there was a higher purpose to what was happening.

But it was hard to embrace the idea because it had "cross" and "crucifixion" written all over it. I thought about how many times I had asked the Lord to conform me to his image, but not once did I have the Passion in mind. To be like Jesus was about gentleness, service, compassion, even power. Not suffering or loss.

The Lord's journey to the cross was now to be my Rosetta stone. The story of his Passion was to guide my response to events I wanted nothing to do with.

Finally, with a deep sense of Christ's call and Presence, I said, *Yes, with your help, Lord.* Responding to opposition the way Jesus did would demand a level of surrender I had never known. I needed to set my eyes on Jesus during what was about to become one of the most formative experiences of my life.

Joy and Suffering

Throughout my life, I had reacted to tough times with two basic responses—flight or fight. That's the way I suffered through night terrors as a child, and it was also the way I lumbered through the long journey of emotional breakdown and recovery. Darkness was my enemy, offering nothing but pain and heartache. My approach had always been to try to kick it in the teeth and then run for my life.

Jesus was asking me to change that strategy. This time, he wanted me to learn how to dance with darkness, promising that it would advance the kingdom in my life and possibly even in my ministry. The idea of trading in my boxing gloves and track cleats for dance shoes seemed absurd. And yet, the Lord promised that if I would seek him in the darkness, new light would shine.

The idea was counterintuitive. Darkness was about evil, and light was the dwelling place of good. It made no sense to be sticking my face into darkness, looking for some treasure that wasn't there. That's the way people get hurt, I thought. Life's great lessons come where the sun is shining, when I could see a long way down the road. Besides, Jesus hung out on mountaintops of transfiguration, where clothes were forever Downy fresh and Clorox white. That's where I longed to be, not tiptoeing on the edge of darkness.

Of course, I knew better than all that drivel. Whether or not I wanted to admit it, my relationship with the Lord had grown whenever Jesus met me in the ditch. I was the guy who was formed by Jesus in a psychiatric hospital and then transformed by a trip to California he didn't want to take. Jesus has always been with me in the dark.

I also knew that my ministry of emotional healing had come out of the dark night I had experienced. What I offered people was not shaped by simply researching the behavioral sciences. Most lessons were written from the experiences I had when Jesus took my hand and danced with me in some very dark places.

The principles I learned about emotional healing were not written on a blackboard but forged in the episodic encounters I had with the Lord even when I could hardly set one foot in front of the other. Though I wanted to run from darkness, I had to admit that I spent most of my time teaching others about what I'd learned when the lights went out. Once again I realized that Corrie ten Boom had been right. The object of my greatest pain had become the source of my greatest blessing.

As Jesus held out the cup to me, I realized he was far more committed to my transformation than I was. He was willing to use "all things" to accomplish that task, even the mess at the seminary. I realized that God's love was neither sloppy sentimentality nor a warm fuzzy. There was no I-like-you-do-you-like-me-check-yes-or-no silliness to it. At times his love hit me with the force of an ocean wave in winter. The question was, What posture should I take to keep my feet under me when the tsunami hits?

That is the precise question I posed to John Nordstrom. John is a pastor and counselor from Ottawa, Illinois. We'd met years before in a pastoral renewal program, and I had found him to be a gentle force. His heart for Jesus is huge, his love for people unwavering, and his ability to speak the right word at the right time unnerving. I called John.

The first response John gave to my emotion-laden description of current events was "Ah, a crucifixion is at hand." I almost faked static on the cell phone and hung up. But I knew what he was saying. He assured me that crosses come to those who follow Jesus and that everyone involved, even those who drive in the nails, can experience spiritual formation if they surrender. I got the point. How I responded would matter not just for me but for others.

John didn't sugarcoat a thing. Neither did he advise escape routes or backup plans as some of my friends had done. Instead, he encouraged me to face into the storm just as the Lord did when he journeyed toward Jerusalem. Not easy, he said, but important for whatever unknown future Jesus had in mind for me.

I posed a question to John. "What posture should I take through this?"

As only John can do, he hit the ball back into my court. "Say more."

"I get that the Lord is saying there is formation in this cup. But I'm not sure whether to be happy or sad about the whole thing."

"That's your answer," John said.

I paused, wondering if he had misheard me. I had posed a question, not provided an answer. But as he left me in that awkward space where words are left unspoken, I got it. The answer was contained in the question. The best posture for me to take was to be happy and to be sad.

To drink the cup, I had to hold joy in one hand and suffering in the other. The creative tension would keep me dead center in the will of God. That's how Jesus walked out the Passion. The Bible says he endured the suffering while setting his heart on the joy that was yet to come. Joy and suffering were held in dynamic tension. That was to be the posture that would guide me through the darkness.

What did this mean practically? Regardless of difficulties, which would prove to be many, I had to keep my eyes on Jesus. I began by driving a stake into Psalm 40 where it says, "He . . . heard my cry. He lifted me out of the slimy pit . . . he set my feet on a rock. . . . He put a new song in my mouth." That would be the joy set before me.

I also had to be honest about the losses I was facing. The disappointment over leaving the seminary, being denied my sabbatical, and being publicly disrespected had to be admitted and grieved. I must not stuff my feelings of betrayal or put a pretty face on the heartache. While holding joy in one hand, I had to find a way to tell it like it was. If the psalmist was free to speak in uncensored lament, so was I.

Joy and suffering were the two reins I must hold in creative tension. Let go of either and I would be going in circles. I had to allow myself to feel the deep sadness of more than twenty years at the seminary coming to such an unfriendly end and also to touch the joy of knowing that new adventures were just over the horizon. It was essential that I not run from feelings of abandonment when institutional leaders remained silent. But I could also rejoice when hundreds of people outside the seminary community sent words of affirmation and encouragement my way.

If I pretended all was joy, I would play nice at the cost of stuffing my feelings. Conversely, if I only moaned about the suffering, I would be pulled into a bottomless pit of desolation. Only by holding onto both joy and suffering would I come out on the other side with the treasures God had for me.

Let the Passion Be Your Guide

Precisely how would the story of Christ's Passion guide me through the storm already at gale force at the seminary? Was it possible that events that took place more than two thousand years ago could speak into the grief, betrayal, and rejection I was navigating? I was sure there were examples of Christian virtues that arose from the biblical narrative. But could I look to the story of the Lord's journey to the cross and find direction for my day-to-day challenges?

The answers were shocking.

The chief financial officer of the seminary asked to meet with me. Upset about what was taking place, he shared information that revealed a potential financial and professional downfall for me. He had decided to resign his position on ethical grounds. I was ready to fight. Each of the friends I confided in advised me to seek legal counsel. It appeared to be the best way to protect my family and myself.

I talked to Cheryl and she wisely advised prayer.

So I presented my idea to the Lord. *Lord, it looks like I may be placed at risk in all of this. Apparently I have legal recourse. I was told I have a case and might possibly need to sue.*

His answer came from the Passion narrative. I had the sense that Jesus was saying, *And I could have called ten thousand angels.* I understood what was being said. It was uncomfortably clear. I knew what I had to do—or in this case not do. It wasn't easy, but the Passion had spoken.

One day, as I stood in a classroom waiting for students to finish an exam, I began thinking about all the miscommunication taking place. By now, things were being said that were flat-out false, that my program drained resources from the seminary and had not been officially approved as an institutional priority even though past seminary presidents had warmly embraced it. I wanted a chance to set the record straight publicly. As I gazed out the window, the Spirit reminded me that Jesus was silent before those who accused him. I didn't like it, but I understood. Let the Passion be my guide.

As the weeks and months wore on, my heart grew heavy about the fact that so few people rose up in my defense. One trustee did talk to the person responsible for the mistreatment but was dismissed and disrespected. A colleague said he would address things with the administration if the opportunity ever presented itself. Apparently it didn't.

At one level I understood, because the new administration did not take kindly to pushback. But it hurt. Being defended was important to me. When I shared my concerns with the Lord, he reminded me of Peter and the servant's ear. Jesus wouldn't allow such a defense because he knew the cup had come from the hand of the Father. The Passion spoke.

I worried that I would be seen as a pushover, afraid to stand up for myself. After all, blood in the water tends to attract hungry sharks. If I sat back and allowed this to happen, people would think they could run right over me whenever they liked. I had faced opposition before because of my emphasis on a more dynamic experience of the Holy Spirit as well as on the use of the imagination in prayer. This would only embolden people who wanted to attack me. Right?

Jesus reminded me that God's strength had been unleashed against the forces of evil when he was hanging on a cross in a display of apparent weakness.

Though walking it out was one of the most difficult challenges I ever faced, the Passion came alive. I was meeting Jesus in the midst of drinking the cup I'd been given, and he was changing me.

Father, Please Help

My time at the seminary ended with the force of a lemon meringue pie to my face. After teaching my final course, I cleared out my office and said goodbye to colleagues and students. There was no fanfare. I wasn't invited to take part in the graduation ceremony, as was the tradition for retirees, nor did I get a note from the president acknowledging my many years of service. It was over.

The next week I was speaking on identity security at a large church in Pennsylvania. I was looking forward to helping people take hold of the unshakable certainty of who they are in Christ. I arrived grateful for the opportunity but feeling emotionally spent.

The last eight months had been filled with a steady flow of opposition, misinformation, and loss. I was drinking the cup, and it was taking its toll. I felt weary and uncertain about what the ultimate endgame was with the Lord.

Early Friday morning I took a walk in the crisp spring air. As I walked and prayed, I thought about the key people—trustees and administrators—who had never once contacted me, never asked how I was doing. They hadn't stood up for me like I thought they should have. The fact that those were my expectations didn't mean they were the Lord's.

Hard as I tried, I couldn't let the hurt go, and now my prayers seemed as weak as tissue paper soaked in water. I was drained of energy. Even the small rise in front of me on my walk seemed too tough to climb, but I did so anyway. The Lord told me to look to the Passion. What had I missed?

I stood at the top of the hill and looked across the Cumberland lowlands toward the Ridge-and-Valley Appalachians to the west. The sun had broken through behind me, warming the back of my neck. Tears formed in my eyes. That's when I saw something fresh in the narrative. I imagined Jesus hanging on the cross, weak and spent. I heard him say, *Forgive them, Father.* Could it have been, just maybe, that the Lord was so drained of life that he had to ask the Father to do what he could not? Was it possible that at that moment of weakness, Jesus needed the Father to forgive on his behalf? Immediately, I prayed the most honest prayer I knew: *Father, I can't lift this disappointment. I've tried. I wish it didn't matter, but it still hurts. Father, I need this gone. I want this gone. Please, Father, do what I cannot do and set me free.*

Then I turned and began walking back down the hill. After five steps, it was gone. I felt the oppression leave as suddenly and dramatically as a light being snapped off. I was free, and with that freedom came life. I couldn't wait to tell Cheryl. I was different. The struggle that had worn me down for months was over. I didn't need a thing from anybody. The cup was empty, the journey complete, and the Resurrection light was mine.

Lessons Along the Way

As I reflect on that experience, I realize I went through several different stages.

It began with *resisting.* When I first heard the question, "Can you drink this cup?" I tried scratching and clawing my way to a different path. Even in the midst of my struggles, I never experienced anything but the Lord's loving patience.

After a while, kicking against the goads nicked me up enough to motivate me to give in. But it was far more *resignation* than surrender. I was on a journey not of my own choosing, and I didn't like it one bit.

Resignation then led to *resentment.* I started moaning and complaining until I was blue in the face. But I never once felt guilty about the harangue. It was a stage I needed to pass through. I was being honest and trusted the Lord enough to believe it was okay.

After that I was able to *relinquish* the storm to the Lord, to open my hand to the all-things plan of God. I no longer saw the trouble as something I had to run from, even though I knew it was dark and unfair. Instead, I learned to dance on the edge with God. I knew that the light of his Presence could penetrate the darkness and that what was meant for bad can be used by him for good. Most of all, I experienced the truth of what Scripture teaches—that following Jesus involves both a cross and a resurrection.

By all appearances I had lost. My seminary career had ended, and the true account of what had happened didn't circulate, at least not in my hearing. In the midst of seeming defeat, I experienced the last stage, which was *rest.* I was able to rest in the Presence of God, knowing he was working everything to the good.

Steve's comments about how I had changed rang true. There was something different about me now. Learning how to dance with God in the midst of my suffering had mysteriously birthed new peace and deeper acceptance in my life. There was something in this trouble I had needed.

Eighteen

LAMENT

Once a month Mom would drag me away from my Saturday morning TV westerns to the neighboring village of Rankintown in order to visit Aunt Bess and Uncle Harry. Their son Carrot and his wife, Evelyn, lived next to them in a neighborhood of side-by-side houses perched directly on the curb. Hard as it was to leave behind Roy Rogers and Gene Autry, it was even harder to be relegated to the living room with Uncle Harry while Mom, Aunt Bess, and Evelyn spent the day cooking, baking, and catching up on the latest gossip.

A kid my age should have relished the chance to spend time with a friendly old gentleman who had fought in the war and hunted every stretch of woods in the county. Not me. I dreaded walking into that room. It wasn't that Uncle Harry was mean, but there were two things about him that gave me the creeps. First, he was a chain-smoker. Handling pack after pack of unfiltered Pall Malls had turned his uncut nails as yellow as his few remaining teeth. I found it hard not to fixate on them.

Even worse was Uncle Harry's big toe. Diabetes had caused a large, hideous-smelling sore to form. He sat in his chair with his foot elevated and his flaky red toe sticking straight out for me to see. According to Uncle Harry, the toe would fester less if he kept it uncovered.

Over time, as the decay crept up his foot and then spread to his leg, I found it hard to stop gawking. I wanted to vomit from the smell of all that rotting flesh. The doctor finally convinced Uncle Harry to have his leg amputated but not before I submitted to the torture countless times.

After that it was only a matter of fighting off the urge to stare at Uncle Harry's stump. When a sore developed on his other foot, another long and putrid journey to a second stump began. During each visit, just when I thought I couldn't take another minute, Aunt Bess would parade in with a tray of food for lunch. Enough said.

Had I not been on sensory overload and fighting to survive, I'm sure I would have felt more compassion for poor Uncle Harry. Along with all the other crazy-making events of my childhood, my time with him contributed to the freak show going on in my head. If something smelled funny, I was sure the odor would stick to me like gum on a shoe. I was certain that no amount of soap and water could cleanse the scent that followed me home.

If anything looked the least bit abnormal, I was toast. My slightly twisted imagination would fixate on sights that engaged my gag reflex, like food hanging on someone's face or the leftover shrapnel of a sneeze gone wild. It could happen anywhere. When it did, Mom would cuff me on the back of the head and tell me to quit staring, even though I couldn't.

Whenever such thoughts locked on, nothing could release the madness in my underdeveloped juvenile brain. It's hard to express how happy I felt that such irrational behavior did not follow me into adulthood. Or so I thought.

Life's Curveball

For years I stood back from my mother and father because of their unpredictable behavior. Mom's temper and fits of meanness cut deep when I was a child. Dad was too busy trying to recapture what was taken from his life to be interested in mine. There came a day when I built walls to escape further hurt. Drawing close seemed dangerous, so I lived respectfully at an arm's reach.

A few years ago, everything changed. While walking to the backyard one sunny afternoon to cut daisies for the dining room table, both Mom and Dad fell. A neighbor discovered them floundering in the grape arbor and crying out for help. Dad was sprawled out on the ground with a back injury while Mom was writhing in pain from a broken ankle. Clearly, their days of living on their own were numbered.

Though I wrestled with the decision, I brought my elderly parents to live in an assisted living facility near my home in Ohio. I had no idea what taking responsibility for their care would demand. There were unanswered questions and truckloads of anxiety.

Mom and Dad would need help with finances, legal issues, medical care, transportation, government paperwork, and countless other things. It was a heavy load, but that wasn't what bothered me. What triggered my anxiety was that the safety wall I had built between us might be jeopardized. I chafed at the deeper relinquishment this might require. As I considered the future, the only thing I could see was trouble headed my way.

A Sacred Space

Mom and Dad had hardly settled into their assisted-living apartment in Ashland before my mother's health rapidly declined. Though they had spent the last seventy-two years together, her journey into the ravages of Alzheimer's disease forced me to make the gut-wrenching decision to separate them. Dad stayed on in the assisted-living apartment alone while Mom moved into the nursing center, sharing a room with a woman she met new every morning.

Mom's illness offered me a front-row seat to what Nancy Reagan had called the long goodbye. Memories fell to the ground like fall leaves as my mother traveled that dreadful journey into dementia. From occasional confusion to complete disorientation. A broken hip, broken ribs, a nasty fall in the bathroom, stitches, and several hospitalizations—until she was wheelchair bound in a lockdown facility.

When my mother was awake, she spent her time mumbling disjointedly about the distant past, engaging events from decades ago as if they had happened yesterday. Mom knew Dad but didn't always recognize the rest of us.

At first I hated spending time in the Alzheimer's care center. When I arrived, Mom would be sitting with other residents near the nursing station. Though they were living in the best-run facility in the area, all of them would be wearing bibs decorated with mementos from their previous meal. I had to stop going at mealtime because I struggled when she incessantly spit food into her lap. This behavior, combined with the smell of urine, challenged my previous conviction that I had grown past childhood sensory foolishness. Apparently my gag reflex had not dissipated with age.

Most days I watched her sleep. Mom seldom remembered those visits, nor did she seem to care. Whenever she was conscious, I listened carefully as she mumbled pieces of disconnected stories from her life.

Though my presence may not have registered, just being there began to restore something inside me. Gradually, the barriers I had placed between us began to erode. The gift of her last years dissolved my defenses, offering an unencumbered view of her wounded heart and terrible childhood. For the first time, I began to consider the full force of Mom's traumatic upbringing. What must it have been like to live as an orphan with relatives who neither wanted nor accepted her?

Instead of labeling her an abusive mother, I began to see her as a little girl swallowed up by grief and loss. Why hadn't I touched the child in her years earlier? No longer hurt *by* her, I started to hurt *for* her, wishing I could travel across time to make things better.

Hand-Me-Down Loss

My mother was born in 1927 in Elrama, Pennsylvania, a coal and steel town on the banks of the Monongahela River. Her father, Wilber Spencer, was part of a clan that had emigrated from Scotland in the mid-nineteenth century. They were decent people, not particularly religious but hardworking and clannish.

Her mother was Edith Boss, the daughter of German immigrants. When Mom was seventeen months old, Edith contracted tuberculosis and died. Even though she didn't have a single memory of her mother, Mom spoke of her often. Losing her was my mother's greatest loss.

After that, she and her father shared a bedroom in his parents' house so that Grandma Spencer could help raise her. Five years later her dad died from renal failure. His body was laid out in the bedroom Mom and he had been sharing, a room she never slept in again. She remembered relatives filling the house for the wake and an old man calling her to his side to give her a stick of gum.

A few years later, when my mother was fourteen, Grandma Spencer fell ill with peritonitis. When she died, Mom's last hope for tenderness was ripped from her, leaving her to live in a downstairs bedroom with her aging grandfather.

Though she talked about these deaths, Mom spoke of them as events rather than as losses that had deeply touched her life. Perhaps she was afraid to let the tears start flowing lest she wind up crying for the rest of her life.

Chronic abandonment kept Mom in perpetual emotional upheaval, which helped to explain why she fought wildly and with military determination to bring everyone under her authority. It also explained her inability to feel empathy and her tendency toward explosiveness.

These traits had kept my sister and me in a state of perpetual hypervigilance, trapped in the paralyzing in-between of come close and get away. We could never predict what we might face—a warm embrace, a stinging silence, an emotional onslaught, or physical abuse. Mom's abandonment wounds and insecure attachment led to our own dysfunction, strangling what each of us needed most in the world.

Considering all the pain of the past, I couldn't have predicted that a nursing home would ever become sacred space. But Mom's did. While Alzheimer's robbed her of her story, it gave back part of mine. Strangely, what was stolen from her opened a treasure box for me that brought healing to our relationship. Anger was replaced by compassion; distance turned to intimacy; and offense stepped aside so forgiveness could do its work.

I had wanted to run from the job of caring for my elderly parents. But now I realized that Mom and I were supposed to walk the last steps of her journey together.

Waves of Grace, Waves of Grief

I was speaking at a seminar in Colorado when news came that Mom had died. Her death hit me harder than I thought it would. I had spent more than three years visiting her almost daily, and suddenly she was gone. Feelings rolled through in waves: sadness and joy, sorrow and gratitude, regret and peace.

Preparations were made for services back in Pennsylvania, which triggered memories of other funerals, none of them good. I had always hated our family's rituals around death. During the course of a three-day wake, people would gather around the corpse in all its ashen glory, talking for hours and in ways that were not always edifying. Then the deceased would be treated to a long funeral during which she would be feted and commended into the hands of the Almighty to be ushered into heaven, regardless of how she had lived. As a child, I thought these rituals dragged on forever. They seemed ghoulish, like something straight from the *Addams Family* playbook.

Thoughts of seeing Mom laid out in a coffin while people lined up to say how nice she looked put my anxiety into overdrive. Pulling up to the front door of the mortuary, I turned to Cheryl and, with a forlorn look and my most pitiful voice, asked, "Do I have to?"

Opening the car door and without a backward glance, she said, "Get out of the car." Though I did as I was told, beneath my best blue suit I was a mess.

If grace is defined as gifts to the undeserving, then what I experienced during those three days in Pennsylvania was lavish love poured out on a flawed man. A steady rain of soft surprises redefined my experience with the traditions surrounding death. I came away with a broadened perspective of the importance of gathering with friends and family at such a time. More importantly, grace opened my eyes to see my mother in a better light.

People came to me as if under divine instruction to share stories and express their affection for my mother. Muriel Spencer, Mom's cousin, wept at the wake and pulled me nose to nose to say, "She was one special lady. I'll miss her. Did you know that when I gave birth to Raymond in 1953, it was your mother who took me to the hospital since Ray Sr. was fighting in Korea? Norma was there for me for more than seventy years!"

Ken Varner, her pastor and neighbor, was moved to tears when he talked about Mom. "She and your dad were the best neighbors. They were like grandparents to our two girls. Your mother helped us in ways no one will ever know. You were sure lucky to have her as your mother." He repeated the whole tribute when he gave the benediction. After the "amen" he squeezed in one final word. "Norma was one special lady."

Every comment was an act of consolation, removing the fog that had formed over my eyes about my mother. Each memory expanded my view of her.

The Final Lesson of the Day

After the funeral, a dark-haired women in her early forties approached, offering her condolences. She acted as though we were long-lost friends. Though it was clear she had known Mom well, I couldn't place her. Recognizing my awkwardness, she said, "Terry, I'm Chris Hensley, Dale's wife."

I smiled in embarrassment. Chris and Dale had lived in my parent's neighborhood for the past twenty years, though time and distance had fogged my recollection of them. As she walked away, a memory surfaced from years earlier. Chris's in-laws, Harlan and Mary Hensley, had lived in the house near my parents, with an undeveloped empty lot separating them. The Hensleys were transplants from rural West Virginia, who had moved to town during the early sixties.

After Harlan died, Mary decided she had room in her heart for two foster children. Six-year-old Lisa and five-year-old Kenny, both from impoverished homes, moved in and became part of her family. Mary figured she'd have love to spare for two developmentally delayed children who were starved for affection.

The two children became fast friends with my niece, who spent every day at our house while my sister was at work. The three ran between the two houses like they owned them. I expected to see each of them playing in the yard or sitting at the kitchen table whenever I came home from college. They were like family, even calling Mom by a title she loved, Grandma Norma.

Kenny was hyperactive and didn't respond well to limits. If you asked him to slow down, he sped up; asked to come here, he ran away; asked to not touch, he grabbed with both hands. He broke more things in the house than I can list.

Short for his age and skinny as a paper clip, Kenny sported cinnamon hair that hung in his eyes and a perpetual crust around his nose. He was fifty-plus pounds of perpetual motion, quick as a squirrel on caffeine. He was a lovable little guy, tenderhearted and unusually affectionate. I remember watching him laugh one day as he tried to spray my mother with the garden hose. As Mom hollered threats fiery enough to make a grown man blush, Kenny giggled like a boy set free.

One night the phone rang. Mom was on the line. What she said hit me like a sucker punch to the gut. "Terry, Kenny was killed by a car today. I can't talk, but I wanted you to know." Then the line went dead.

The accident had happened midmorning while Mom was sweeping off the back porch and neighbors were puttering around their houses, taking care of their own chores. Dad was getting his work clothes out and lunch bucket ready so he could head to the mine for second shift. Every so often a car would drive by.

The softness of that sunny June morning was shattered when Mary Hensley burst through her front door and screamed, "Grandma Norma, Kenny's been hit by a car." Mary bolted down the porch steps, ran across the corner of her lawn, and frantically darted toward the top of Norman Avenue, all the while yelling, "No, no, no!"

Kenny had been told never to ride his bike in the street. Since he was still unsteady on a two-wheeler, Mary was adamant that he should stay on their paved driveway, not venturing one foot onto the road in front of their house. But with Mary inside, Kenny couldn't resist the temptation to ride his bike the short distance to the top of the hill, turn around, and then glide back down into the driveway. Easy enough.

What Kenny didn't know was that an elderly woman was driving her Plymouth Fury up the road just as he was starting down. Because of her habit of creeping along slowly, other drivers dreaded getting caught behind her. Most would get frustrated, blowing their horns in hopes of getting her to speed up or pull over. That morning, just as she was cresting the hill, she struck Kenny head on as he swerved into her path. Oblivious of having hit anything, the woman dragged him under her car all the way to the stop sign.

Horrified by what they'd just witnessed, neighbors ran alongside the car banging on the door, begging her to stop. But it was too late. Kenny and his bicycle were twisted under the car, mangled beyond recognition.

My mother ran up the road and arrived minutes after it happened. People were gathered around the car, some shouting at the driver, others walking back and forth in shock. Mary Hensley was on her knees crying frantically. Mom pushed past everyone, got down on her knees, and looked under the car to find Kenny.

Then she got on her belly, twisted her head to the side to avoid the exhaust pipe, and used her hands and feet to scoot herself as far up beneath the car as possible. Pushing debris out of the way, she found Kenny's hand. Lying in the blood and dirt, she held onto his small fingers while he breathed his last. There was no way that little boy was going to die alone. Mom was determined to show him that someone who loved him was with him.

Why didn't I remember this example of my mother's devotion and determination—a story of heroic proportion that remained hidden in my mind for forty years? Why had I never reflected on what that story said about Mom's character? And why did so many of the positive anecdotes I heard as I stood beside her casket take me by surprise? How could I have focused on desolate and dark memories to the exclusion of all that was good about her? Emotional wounds had kept me from appreciating the whole story of her life. But now I knew that she was greater than my experience of her.

Waves of grace in a time of grief altered the story that I had believed for most of my life. Though I understood how deeply Mom had hurt me, new, more loving memories emerged as God adjusted my angle of vision.

Nineteen

BELOVED

The early morning sun was chasing the shadows down mountains to the west. Seated in an overstuffed chair, I gazed through a sweeping wall of windows to take in the breathtaking vistas that only the Rockies can provide. To the north, glider pilots from the US Air Force Academy were taking off and landing like bees from a hive. On the interstate below, cars rushed bumper to bumper, as if the drivers were already late for work.

The noise at my back reminded me that the event staff at the World Prayer Center in Colorado Springs was getting ready for the day. They were busy placing resources on tables and testing the sound system as the worship team gathered on stage for a quick rehearsal. Caregivers were in the corner of the room praying. My administrative assistant, Lynne, was flitting about like a hummingbird, consumed with last-minute preparations.

I was surrounded by people who gave the impression there was nowhere else they would rather be. Counselors, pastors, physicians, psychologists, and educators had joined me as part of a team of people specially trained to position hurting people for Christ's healing. Most would not mind being referred to as wounded healers.

As two hundred people filed in and found their seats, I reflected on the fact that I'd done seminars like this one nearly a hundred times over the course of the last twenty years. During each one, I had talked about my story and invited participants on a journey to wholeness with Christ. Nearly every time, a familiar question would form in my mind. *How did a guy from a background of verifiable weirdness and debilitating wounding get the privilege to talk so much about Jesus and see lives wonderfully transformed?*

I smiled because the answer was always the same. *Love.* God's love was furious in its determination to set me free, to release me from bondage, and to exchange the shame I had carried for an inheritance of joy.

My Life

If life were more like math, mine wouldn't add up to what it has thus far. The sum of my parts doesn't equal the life I've been given to live. I suppose that's true for anyone who has been transformed by Christ.

After giving up on my own small agenda, I discovered that the ultimate goal of my life was neither to be healed nor even to be used, but to be completely enfolded in the embrace of Father, Son, and Holy Spirit. I can never forget that my journey toward deeper union began not when I was pursuing security through performance but when I was allowing Jesus to guide me on that greatest of all adventures—the one that happened as I moved from broken to beloved. Union with God has become both my highest goal and greatest good, just as it should be for everyone who belongs to him.

I am a blessed man, married to my high school sweetheart who is even more attractive than the day we met. Cheryl and I live on a beautiful farm and enjoy the support of close friends. I have three adult children who serve the Lord and a daughter-in-law and two sons-in-law who have stolen my heart. We cherish our amazing grandchildren.

I have been privileged to serve as a pastor of growing churches and as a seminary professor for three decades. God has helped me develop a method of healing prayer used by thousands of people around the world. I've written books and spoken across the country. By all accounts I live an enviable life.

Considering where I began and all the pain along the way, my story should be quite different—with far more tragedy than comedy. But grace came down and swept me up into the greater story of Jesus and his love. That same grace brought others in its wake, which makes me shake my head in wonder.

I won't forget the day I shared the message of Jesus with Grandma Mose. Given the take-no-prisoners life she had lived, I couldn't imagine how she would respond.

"I guess I have been waiting my whole life to hear that," she said to me. Then, in that stale living room with its hideous green walls and with tears streaming down her face, she knelt and met Jesus. The next Sunday she went to church for the first time in her long life and never missed a Sunday after that until she moved into a nursing home.

Years after retiring from the coal mine, Dad surprised me by saying he was taking voice lessons because he wanted to sing in church. He joined the choir, became an usher, and even served on the trustee board. Though he never said much about the emotional abandonment that had characterized my childhood, we grew closer once he moved to Ashland.

I was in Colorado the day Mom died, but I was able to talk to her. As my sister held the phone to my mother's ear, I spoke about my love, assuring her it would be okay to leave us. I told her Jesus would soon reach out his hand, and when he did she should take it because she was going home. In less than an hour, she let go of life to arrive safe and sound on the other side. I miss her but I know she's well.

The outpouring of God's grace over the course of my journey flung open the door for a closer relationship with my father-in-law as well. I remember how surprised I'd been when he told me he wanted to pay for my doctorate. Later, grace made a way for me to help him when he was dying of bone cancer. I'll never forget him lying on the couch, sick and in pain, and saying, "I'm glad you're here, Son." It was never "Terry" anymore but always "Son." What a long way from that day when he strapped on his .38!

Always a gold-medal sister, Bonny became a Christ follower too. Stunned that her little brother had turned out okay, she even attended a couple of my seminars. My kids adore their devoted aunt.

Though it took awhile, many other relatives came around too, not so jumpy anymore about me being a "preacher," as they called me. Grace makes impossible things happen all the time.

I can't believe I have this life. So many stories set in motion from the grace awakening of a crazy kid from the wrong side of town. Because of God, I get to live an adventure every day. Instead of trying to figure out how I got here, I've decided to just keep heading down the road to the next surprise. Sometimes, in the middle of thanking Jesus for everything he's done, I think I hear him whisper, *Terry, you ain't seen nothin' yet!*

Two Tables

Students have sometimes asked me to name the single most important truth I've learned on my journey. It's hard to pick a favorite when the answer could be as simple as "Jesus loves me; this I know" or as complex as the writings of Thomas Aquinas. These days I talk a lot about the two tables that are set before us, each one offering very different answers about what it means to be fulfilled.

Throughout my life I have been driven by deep longings placed in my heart by God. I have ached for love and belonging, looking for people who would not just accept me but who would give the impression that the party didn't begin until I arrived. Though I couldn't have articulated these longings at the time, they were what sent me across the street every day of my childhood in search of Grandma Mose's embrace and Uncle Fat's ornery but affectionate welcome.

As I grew, the longing for significance grew right along with me.

I needed to know that my existence mattered and that there was a purpose to my life, which someone would help me to discover and shape. Finding my place with Carrot's hunting pals and hanging out with the grease-stained gang at the Venetia garage was a start. More than anything, I desperately needed to be secure, to find a solid place to stand when the wind and waves tried to wipe me out.

Looking back I see that much of my story was about killing the pain of those longings when they went unmet or trying to meet them in any way possible, regardless of who I stepped on along the way. I wish I had been strong enough to say no to the trip to the Green Man, the PCP-induced nightmare at Dairy Queen, and the temptation to compromise some really nice people just to calm the storm in my own soul. I wasn't.

The Table of the World

The first table I invested in, the one that is offered to everyone, is what I call the table of the world. Many of the items on that impressive-looking table promised to fulfill the deepest longings of my life. Carnival hawkers stood alongside shouting out slogans about money, power, possessions, and privilege, assuring me that if I played their game, I would be a winner. Investing my identity there would turn me into a somebody.

The assumption at this table was that I was not enough. In order to be loved, to feel secure, or to have a sense of significance, I had to be more than I was. That entailed working hard to measure up to the preferred standards of achievement. The degree to which I achieved would determine the degree to which I received.

The standards differed depending on the context. In my hometown, measuring up was determined by how much alcohol I drank, how well I hunted, how many girlfriends I had, and whether I could fight my way out of a fix. On the athletic field it was about hits and home runs or baskets and fast breaks. In academics it came down to grades and degrees or awards and titles. Every context had its own Howdy Doody yardstick.

The table of the world valued pleasing and performing. It was a place for conducting transactions. If I . . . , then they. *Doing,* rather than *being,* was the only currency worth trading. But having a seat at this table was always conditional. If I failed to please or perform at adequate levels, I no longer got to sit down. This table kept me running because I knew I could lose my seat faster than I had won it. Despite its allure, there was no security at the table of the world.

I had invested deeply, whether with the good old boys at home or the nose-in-the-air academic crowd. I longed for a place at the table, ached to sit where the deepest cries of my heart might be satisfied. Fighting to get a seat at that table produced a lot of anxiety and fear. Anger soon followed. Over time, the table of the world became for me a place of desolation, not hope. Striving for a place there had cost me dearly, leaving me with nothing. Its promises were as empty as cream puffs without the cream.

Somewhere along the way a cross and Bible got placed on that table and the table was renamed "Christian." Though the nature of achievement changed, the fundamental message was the same: *You don't measure up. You need to try harder, pray harder, read the Bible more, serve more. Maybe, if you do all these things, you might get to sit down, at least for a little while. Maybe.*

I didn't realize that performance-based faith is nothing more than a business deal. God has something you want—eternal life. You have something he wants—holy living. If you give him what he desires, he will deliver what you want. It's like a vending machine. Put in the right amount of money and out comes a soda. To receive, I had to first give. But in my broken-down state, I had nothing to give.

Though I tried to sit at various versions of the same table, I ended up in the ditch instead.

The Table of the Lord

When I fell down the ladder of success and then all the way down into a psychiatric breakdown, many of my colleagues stepped away from me lest they be contaminated by my failure, considered guilty by association. Unable to perform to the prescribed standards, I no longer belonged at their table, and nobody wanted to join me in the ditch.

Fortunately, I discovered that Jesus has no fear of ditches. In fact he does some of his best work with people who find themselves there. It was in the midst of such an experience that the Father called me his son and set a banquet before me. After I failed miserably, he blessed me lavishly. For the first time, I began to understand that Jesus had crossed the universe not to conduct a business transaction but to invite me into a relationship. No wonder the Pharisees were so scandalized by Jesus's table manners. They judged him harshly for sharing a meal with people like me who hadn't been playing by the rules!

Ever so slowly I began to realize that God doesn't treat his children like the world treats people. When I was washed out and washed up, the Father brought out rings and robes and fatted calves. My identity as God's child, not my behavior, was what afforded me a permanent seat at his table. He lavished his love on me because I belonged to his family.

Everything I longed for was available at the table of the Lord. More love? I could find it at the table. A deeper sense of belonging? It was there at the table. Purpose, understanding, significance, even security could be found as I sat down at the table of the Lord and ate. I would never need to present a list of accomplishments or photos of all my possessions. Nor would I need to demonstrate how good I was or remind the Lord of my last best performance. In fact, these things had to be left at the door because they meant nothing at God's table.

Sitting at the table of the Lord was about believing that Jesus had drawn me into a relationship with the Father. It was about knowing I was part of the family. My security came from my identity as his son. That's what gave me a permanent place at the table. I began to rest in the fact that I didn't earn my seat through strength and would never lose it through weakness. It wasn't about how I was doing but about what Jesus has done.

Striving for a seat at the table of the world had cost me everything. My seat at the table of the Lord had cost Jesus everything. He gave his life to make me a child of the Father. I had standing in his family, which meant that God would satisfy the deepest longings of my life.

I remember the day I got lost in Psalm 23. I was praying through a valley of sadness as my time at the seminary was coming to a close. The phrase "The Lord is my shepherd" was drawing me into the heart of Christ. I imagined him setting a rich table in front of all the people who had screamed that I was not enough. Watching him pull out a chair, I smiled when he invited me to sit down with no questions asked. Not once did he bring up my past or ask about my accomplishments. Neither was he curious about my most recent failure. He simply invited me to sit at his table.

Holding a cup in his hand, he asked if I was thirsty. When I nodded, he took a pitcher of wine and began to pour. I expected him to stop once the wine had filled the cup, but Jesus kept pouring as it spilled over the lip of the cup, staining the tablecloth, dripping down on the ground, and saturating the soil beneath my feet.

Looking into his eyes, I saw joy, not waste. Jesus was showing me the scandalous generosity of kingdom grace—abundant, overflowing, extravagant, unthinkable, and incomparable. That's when I heard words that sealed the truth in my heart about what it's like to sit forever at the table of the Lord: *This type of goodness and love will follow you all the days of your life, and you will rest here forever because this is your home, my son.*

It's About the Foundation

I'd never seen a photo of myself with Grandpap until a short 8 mm clip of the two of us was recently discovered by a relative digging through a box of photos. After transferring the film to a thumb drive, I wept when I viewed those images.

Grandpap is digging out the foundation for Carrot and Evelyn's new house in Rankintown. The whole village has turned out to watch and help. I recognize Dad, Bonny, Mom, Evelyn, Jimmy, and Aunt Bess. Uncle Harry is navigating the building site in his wheelchair.

I can almost smell the mix of diesel fuel and dirt wafting through the air as great mounds of soil are bitten from the ground and placed to the side. Black smoke billows from the stack as the tractor walks on steel crawlers, the engine noise drowning out the boisterous chatter of the crowd gathered around the rim to watch.

Grandpap stops the bulldozer and motions for Dad to bring me down. Then he hikes me up so I can nestle between his legs, my head resting on his sweaty chest. Though I am only four years old, I have become the envy of every kid in the crowd. When Grandpap shows me how to work the levers, I am as proud as the king of Siam. My little fingers clutch the leather grips as I navigate back and forth moving dirt. I thought it was all my doing, but of course Grandpap is pulling the cables, digging deep to be sure the new house will be built on a solid foundation.

That ancient film clip made me think about the importance of foundations. Most people pay far more attention to the things that make a house attractive and comfortable—windows, carpets, room size, paint, lighting, and window treatments. How many of them would direct everyone's attention to the foundation while giving a tour of a new home? Not many, especially since most of the foundation is hidden in the dirt.

But foundations matter. If you don't dig beneath the frost line and construct a concrete footer that is both wide and deep, the house is headed for trouble. Once when I was working with a crew putting sheeting on a roof, the foundation gave way and shifted the house. A boatload of time and money didn't put it quite right.

Compromise on the foundation and every other investment in the house is at risk.

Every house Grandpap ever built was constructed on a firm foundation. Not so his life. Living hard on a fractured identity meant that he hurt himself and a lot of other people. I was headed for the same disaster, building for the heights while the depths were being ignored. I was my grandfather's grandson.

Like Grandpap, I ended up crashing hard, but in a different way. The deconstruction I needed to endure wasn't fun, especially when a lot of what I had built had to be tossed on the burn pile. But the reconstruction has been a profound adventure of grace as the Lord secured my identity on the solid rock of his acceptance and love.

A huge part of me still loves the place where I grew up and the people who populated that gritty corner of the world. I like to think that I am carrying on a tradition that goes all the way back to that day on the bulldozer. Only this time I am sitting in the lap of God.

Just like then, I sometimes think I'm the one doing all the work, when deep inside I know it's him.

Transformation didn't come because I did everything right, was healed every time I prayed, or because God used me. It happened and still happens as I surrender to his love day by day. That's the path we are all called to take. As we stay on the journey, we'll look back with wonder, recognizing that God has used our brokenness to help us understand just how beloved we are.

Acknowledgments

This story began long before I was born. But the book was birthed the day Ann Spangler introduced herself and said, "I'm a literary agent and would love to work with you to tell your story." Work she did—not only to help me connect with the right publisher but also to improve my writing, help focus the narrative, and encourage me through more than a few rough spots. Ann is the velvet-covered brick, determined to bring the best out of me so that people who are hurting will be touched by the healing Presence of Christ. I cannot thank her enough.

John Sloan is a master writing coach who has become a cherished friend. His ability to find the narrative arc in my story and keep me moving along that path were essential to this project. He had "eyes to see and ears to hear" when I could barely find the forest for the bark. I was humbled that he would choose to work with me and am hoping for more days to come when we sit at the table and dream.

I have been thrilled to work with the wonderful people from WaterBrook. Special thanks to my editors, Bruce Nygren, Ingrid Beck, and Pamela Shoup who invested deeply in the project. Also, I want to express my gratitude to Johanna Inwood, Chelsea Woodward, and Beverly Rykerd of the marketing and publicity teams, as well as Mark Ford and Kristopher Orr in cover design. They each know the meaning of above and beyond.

I want to extend special thanks to Lynne Lawson, executive coordinator of Healing Care, LLC. She was willing to place more on her plate so that I could concentrate on writing. She has, for almost two decades, been invaluable in more ways than I am able to express. Lynne is the "one in a million." Thanks also to the Healing Care administrative and program staff: Kim Moraghan, Michael O'Hara, Peter Burgo, Jeff Franks, and Aaron and Destry Wardle.

Thank you also to the many people who make up the Healing Care family. They are the salt of the earth, wounded healers who love to position the broken for healing encounters with Christ. These healers extended lots of grace to me despite the crooked path I have walked toward Jesus. They heard many of these stories long before I decided to write them down in a book. There are too many names to include, but from the depths of my heart I say, "Your love has changed me!"

My sister, Bonny, has been a constant source of love in my life, even when times were tough. While I was writing this book, Bonny sat for hours verifying stories, recalling details I had forgotten, and filling in blanks in the long narrative of our family history. We laughed, cried, and shared the hope that people will connect to Jesus through my story.

At this writing my dad, Puz Wardle, is still living and is well into his nineties. For several years, and even more so since Mom's home going, I have sat and asked questions that sparked story after story, many of which are contained in this book. Like me, Dad has journeyed toward Jesus over the rocky road that has been his life. I am grateful that in the twilight of Dad's life, God has brought a new day in our relationship.

My son, Aaron, and my daughters, Cara and Emily, have relentlessly loved me despite the road burn my journey left on me. They have had front-row seats to the miracle of transformation that God has performed. They have also been a welcoming sanctuary, playing a part in my story that cannot be overstated. The word *thanks* is simply inadequate for these three, who are God's works of art. Thanks also to my daughter-in-law, Destry, and my sons-in-law, Brad and Micah. You are gifts.

My grandchildren contribute to my life in ways they cannot comprehend. What others might consider interruptions to the writing process I experienced as miracles in the midst of the mundane. Whenever I sat at the computer writing and heard, "Papa, can you come and . . ." I heard an invitation to an adventure with the most precious people on the planet. So, to Grace, Addi, Kayla, Caleb, Ella, and Charlotte, thanks, and remember that Papa is nuts about you!

I want to thank the first and forever love of my life, Cheryl. Over half a century has passed since we stepped out on our first date, on New Year's Eve, 1967. Since then, with many ups and downs, victories and defeats, times of great pain and incredible joy, we have come to a spacious and sacred space together. Cheryl, your love is oxygen for my soul! I thank you for reading the many drafts of this manuscript and for holding me close as I unearthed old pain. The words "You complete me" could not be more true. Indeed, you are perfect for me!

It is my hope that Jesus will find a way to shine through these pages with grace and healing light. It is no secret that he can change a life, even one as wounded and crazy as mine. Instead of crossing his arms and waiting for us to get on the right path, he extends his arms on the cross so that we can find freedom on freedom's side. Two things are certain: I'm still on the journey, and there is always room for one more.

Terry's Ministry

Terry's story, though unique, is not an isolated example of emotional wounding. Countless people struggle with unprocessed emotional pain, which invariably impacts what they believe about themselves, the way they relate to other people, and how they view God.

Emotional wounding can be debilitating and crosses barriers of race, gender, age, class, ethnicity, education, and religion. It is present among followers of Christ, keeping countless believers from living free on freedom's side.

For two decades, thousands of people have attended events sponsored by Terry's organization Healing Care, encountering Christ and experiencing emotional healing. His seminars equip professional and lay caregivers to position broken people for emotional healing, as well as empower everyday Christians to live free on their journey toward Christ.

Opportunities include basic and advanced seminars in formational prayer, certificate programs in formational prayer and spiritual direction, and events on topics such as "Awakening to the Unshakable Certainty of Who You Are in Christ," "Becoming People of the Presence," "Seeking: Six Questions Jesus Asks to Guide the Christian Journey," "Lord, Teach Us to Pray," and many others.

Through his organization The Healing Care Center, people are able to receive counseling, spiritual direction, healing prayer, and life coaching. There are opportunities for intensive retreats aimed at emotional healing, as well as online resources that serve people on their journeys. Qualified caregivers and counselors join Terry and Cheryl in providing help for the hurting.

Information about the ministry of Healing Care is available through the following platforms, where you will find books, resources, free videos and workbooks, as well as a schedule of upcoming events, including descriptions of the various ministries available.

www.terrywardle.org

https://slingstones.podbean.com/

www.facebook.com/TerryWardleHCM/

https://hcminternational.org/

www.instagram.com/terrywardle_healingcare/